When Life Makes Sense

Exploring the meaning of life through
science, philosophy and faith

A. A. ALEBRAHEEM

This publication is designed to provide general information regarding the subject matter covered. Nothing in this book is meant to be portrayed as medical advice, counselling, or therapy. The contents of this book are for educational purposes only.

www.alebraheembooks.com

ISBN-13: 978-1979876667
ISBN-10: 1979876665

Printed in the United States of America

Table of Contents

Introduction

One day, one of my tutors advised me, "If you ever come across a newspaper blown away by the wind along the road, pick it up and read it. You never know; it might contain a piece of information that could be useful someday". I acted on his advice. In all that I have encountered in my life, I have always paused in order to properly discern all the events and identify their causality. Whenever I stumble upon an incomprehensible matter that I am investigating, or when I come across a word I do not know, I stop and look it up. This is what we all do. We refer to our virtual search engines on the Internet, type in the ambiguous word, suffixed by "meaning of", and off we go to find out the meaning that will make sense out of this word. Today, we want to type in together, "What is the meaning of life?" It wouldn't be right if we were able to grasp whatever we see, and were able to place it in a logical context, while we are still bewildered with regards to the meaning and logical context of the very life that we live.

We all cross the river of life, whether we know the reason for this life or not. Our boat that we sail will carry us along, whether we know the way it sails or not. So, is it important to find a meaning in this life?

Many people live with no understanding of life, and when their boats crash into a disease, a financial loss or the loss of a dear one, they either start reconsidering their life's vision and its meaning, or simply put an end to their own life, because it has become meaningless!

I write to those who are focused on their goals, to those who know where they wish their boat to sail, to those who are curious to understand the direction and the stops of their boat. But I also write to those who never wonder where the river of life is carrying them, and the location that they might end up in.

The waters of the river of this life never stop flowing; just as we came into life, we will be gone, followed by others. Ahead of us have sailed billions of people with their boats, and most likely, many more billions will take that journey after us. When we know the reason behind our being on a boat on the river of life, we will then learn how to sail and where to put in. If we realize this, we will also realize our needs, and choose our sailing companions wisely.

Life is life with all its achievements and disasters, joys and sorrows. We drift along the river of life, with its bends, rocks, and the great waterfall of death. Let us improve our tools and 'telescopes', to be able to foresee the rocks before we get to them. Let's be prepared for the sharp river bends and master the skill of dealing with life's disasters. Whoever does not wonder what the meaning of their being on board the boat of life is, will keep filling it with food because they once starved, or fill their boat with money because they were once impoverished. Have they found out why they are on the boat?

We could write a thousand over-the-top articles, but would never become widely-known writers. When we consult a specialist in writing, he will tell us that the propagation of our essays is not brought about by what we write, but rather by whom we write about. He would advise us to recognize the audience that we are addressing. It is this audience that will share and spread what we have written. Once we have this piece of information, we will have already placed our feet on the first step on the staircase of fame. Nonetheless, the first step on the staircase of fame means that we are second or third-grade authors and this is not enough to enable us to reach the top of the staircase of fame.

At this point, we should determine what the next step should be. We should aim to address a large group of people, the issues that touch their hearts and their souls. When many people read our articles, some of them will definitely share them with others, and this is how our articles would spread.

When we write in this manner for many years, and still don't reach fame, we will need a specialist to review our articles. He may tell us that our topics are important, yet lifeless. The newspaper reader is not the same as the academic reader. The former is searching for a piece of information, yes, but he would more inclined towards the writer who gives him the information in a manner that also provides entertainment. The specialist then, would recommend that our articles become more fun.

When we incorporate some fun into the information, but still don't succeed, we might then visit an incredibly well-known writer and ask him why we have failed to climb to the top of the staircase to fame. He might tell us how he, in his early stages as a writer, had bad-mouthed a celebrity, so he gained notoriety. He might simply have paid for his prominence on social media websites, and so become famous that way. Maybe he had a secret source of information, which enabled him to be the only person writing about a particular subject. When we become a little famous, someone will come by and point us in the direction of further fame.

After becoming really famous, we will still need the specialists to teach us how to make the most of our fame to achieve our financial and social goals. That is how this life works; whoever can see their next move, will be able to achieve it more easily than those who do not know their next move; destined to remain on the same step of their staircase.

The same goes for the meaning of life; we can't get to it without knowing the right moves. Whoever wants to know the meaning of life without knowing the moves that can get him to that meaning is similar to a person who alleges that his ability to read and write is enough for him to become a famous writer.

The first move towards knowing the meaning of life is recognizing the meanings of life that we come in contact with, and there are many. We will recognize our money that keeps us entertained, our life partners and children, along with our unconditional love of them and their love and care for us. There are many other meanings that revolve in our orbits and

4

illuminate our lives. When our feet step onto that step, we will get to know the step of "what is the reason for the existence of these meanings?" which is the following step. Afterwards, we will search for whoever has already tried to answer the question about the meaning of life. We will keep climbing together, the steps of the staircase of the meanings of life, until we touch the meanings of our own life with our hands, and discover the reason why they are revolving in our orbits, and why they are shining. *Then*, we will get to truly know our life and its meanings.

Can You Dance?

At the beginning of my journey as a writer, I wrote for a newspaper. Later, I wrote my first book. Back then, I didn't enjoy writing. I only wrote because I had to. I didn't want to die and have all the knowledge inside my head die with me. Writing used to leave me cold, but I had a need to put my thoughts down on paper. I didn't want my life to end like that of a moth, worthless[1], without giving anything back.

I knew my writing was good, and that I had thoughts and ideas that I needed to share with others. I knew I could choose my role on this earth, and that is why I chose that my role would be a

---

[1] There is no doubt that these harmful creatures have a role in rebalancing the earth, But, I don't want to play that role.

5

useful one. Like a bee that takes the pollen for itself, but makes honey as well. I didn't want my knowledge to remain a prisoner within my mind, that was my sole aim. Making a profit wasn't something I was thinking about. This book you are reading now is the third I have written, and I'm still not interested in making a profit from it. Sharing my thoughts and ideas with you is far more important. I am happy to share my thoughts and ideas with you, with just one condition. As the Egyptian saying goes, "the matter which starts with a condition, ends with light". This is exactly what I am offering you. My condition for you, my reader, is simply to stop reading and put this book down, every time you feel bored. Whether you're bored of reading itself, or you've simply had enough of me! So, can we do this? Keep to this agreement and while it may take more time to get to the end of the book, you'll see the light when you finally get there. So please dear reader(,) abide by my condition. You may be wondering why I am asking for this. Well it is simple; while you read this book, I will be giving you my secrets. I will be talking to you through this book, and it's important that when you read what I have to say to you, that you are in the right frame of mind to take it all in, with positivity, and an open, fresh mind. So that's all you need to do, my one request of you. Simply put this book aside when you begin to feel bored.

I work as a finance controller, and I write after work, on weekends and on my vacations from work. While most of my friends try to have a good time after a week of work, I grab my personal computer and start writing. I haven't visited my vacation house for 7 months, neither have I enjoyed the swimming pool I have over there. It's true that writing didn't use to thrill me; however, my feelings about writing began to improve after I found an influence, an echo and an outcome from what I write, for I write to leave a legacy. When I discovered this influence, it gave me a better feeling about writing more.

When I get into a discussion, I am used to looking for the signals that show me whether the other party is listening or not. When the listening stops, through a loss of focus or distraction, this would most likely be the end of the conversation, and time to change the subject. It doesn't make sense to keep sending signals to someone who has turned off their radio receiver! I cannot feed a "mind" that is already full.

This is the core of the agreement between us. Our conversation together in this book will be like dancing; I will step forward whilst you step back, refrain from thinking, and give me your ear. And when you consider my words, I will step back whilst your thinking advances. Let us stop dancing if the forward and backward movements stop. Standing still cannot be called dancing, and will not lead us to the benefits of the book.

If either of us gets bored of the other's talk, benefit will cease. Let us agree that our journey ought to be enjoyable all through its stages. If the pleasure of the curiosity for knowledge doesn't overwhelm you, and you don't sense a new taste of knowledge within each and every page in my book, you will not feel thrilled.

If you do not feel thrilled, please do not carry on with dancing to the melodies of my book. If the drums of a burning desire to finish this book, just for the sake of finishing or rushing, start beating, ignore them.

Let our desire to benefit remain more important than our desire to enjoy, or the curiosity to know. If we feel bored of each other, let us stay apart, and later, let us come back to conversing with one another when you are in a good mood for reading, and when I am in a good mood for writing; and we go back to a conversation that is like dancing.

A year of my life has gone by while I have been writing the pages of this book, which is no more than 200 pages long. I have been sculpting its ideas like a masterpiece which I have been refining; adding and removing, writing and erasing. I have removed from it more than I have added to it. I didn't rush to get it done. Whenever I had the feeling that my talk was no longer interesting, or I felt bored, I would neglect my writing, and get myself busy with something else until my energy returned to me.

I have written some parts of my book in April 2017, at an altitude of 41,000 feet, on a plane taking me from Los Angeles to my home in Kuwait. I started writing, got bored, and so I watched a movie called *The Edge* starring Anthony Hopkins. After I was done with watching the movie, I felt my energy for writing coming back. And here I am, talking to you again. So, do you have the same amount of energy?

I wrote some other parts of my book in August 2017 on board a ship that stopped at the Geirangerfjord port in Norway. I slipped away from my children, placed my personal computer on a table in the ship, enjoyed the fascinating landscape from the 13th floor, watching the high, green Norwegian mountains, and the waterfalls that sneak through them. On the other side of the mountain, I saw, behind those mountains, yet another mountain totally covered with snow. There was a green valley where some sheep were roaming. I have absorbed a lot of beauty, and have mixed the knowledge of this into the pages of my book with many examples, hoping to make my reader dance as though enchanted. I want you to only read my book when you feel the passion of it, when my words truly speak to you and you yearn for more. If you receive any signals, do not ignore them. Whenever you tell yourself, "I get the point of this page", and you feel like moving on without finishing it, that is one of the signs of boredom. Put my book aside and don't pick it up again except when you feel like going through every paragraph in it once more. If you find the pages of the book lacking consistency, or that you had to reread the text more than once to understand it, all of these are signs that indicate one of two things; either your mental and psychological states are not ready, or there is something wrong with the book that is keeping us from communicating effectively. Let us stop talking, and text me on Twitter (@AlebraheemBooks), or share your thoughts with some former readers of my book, through sites such as Goodreads, or via my website Alebraheembooks.com on any of the reading blogs. You shall find the answer. Afterwards, go back to the page where you left off, so that we can continue our conversation.

My advice is to myself and to you, and it is not concerned exclusively with this book. Reading just one book and deeply understanding it is better than speed reading an entire library. Going through a page again is better than turning to the next. Do we agree then?

Chapter 1

What Is The Meaning?

A meaningful – or a "full-of-meaning" – matter is something that has deep significance. Meaning equates to significance and being worthy of attention[2]. A person whose actions are not deliberate would have these actions described by others as "meaningless", indicating a lack of aim within that person.

Very often, we see some very professional teachers explaining sophisticated and multi-stage topics. After explaining the first stage of the answer, they remind their audience of the importance of what they have learned in the first stage, so as to build on it what they will say subsequently. So, they ask, "What does that mean?" They pause, implant the piece of information and predetermine the direction of the upcoming explanation. So, meaning is almost everything.

Meaning is aim, significance and value. The lack of meaning is the absence of value, significance and aim. If you wish to describe someone as petty, there is no need to address him as a person. It will suffice to tell him that his speech is devoid of any

---

[2] T. Metz, 'The Meaning of Life', The Stanford Encyclopedia of Philosophy (Summer 2013 Edition), Edward N. Zalta (ed.),
https://plato.stanford.edu/archives/sum2013/entries/life-meaning/ (accessed 30 June 2017).

meaning. That should do to make the spectators realize his pettiness.

When we tell someone that their words are deep, they will surely feel flattered. On one side of the coin, meaning is the opposite of pettiness. On the other side, meaning is opposite to valueless. Anything that has no meaning for its existence does not have any value.

The meaning of life that we are in search of cannot be a trivial one. Our life includes our joys that mean a lot to us, and our deep sorrows that take us out of the box of our lives, make us reflect on our lives, and communicate our deep emotions. Our joys make up the diamonds threaded onto the 'necklace' of our lives. Our sorrows are the dark stones of our necklace.

Joy and sorrow make up a mixture that makes us see different meanings in our life, in its pleasures and in our future ambitions. Our great plans for ourselves and for our families have deep and sincere meanings.

The meaning of our lives cannot possibly be of any less importance and sincerity. Thus, we shall search for this meaning and that ultimate goal, which would be the necklace thread that pulls all our targets together, raising our awareness and insight into what we are doing in our lives, and what suits the necklace of our own life and what doesn't.

Do We Need a Definite Meaning to Our Lives?

Before I buy a new medicine, I usually read the enclosed leaflet. When I find out that the risks of using that drug, which are written on the enclosed leaflet, are too many, I start searching the web for reviews written by patients who have used that drug before me. But, the words I use for the search are those that express harm; for instance, "Beware of this medicine", "Disastrous drug" or "Stay away from...". This retrospective search saves me time and gives me the desired results. If I just typed in the drug name and searched for the patients' reviews about it, the journey of reading the information concerned with it would be long.

The same goes for the meaning of life. We will go a long way in order to talk about the importance of the meaning of life. The retrospective search about the lack of meaning in life will take us through a shortcut and give us the same answer to the same question.

Is The Lack of Meaning in Life Harmful?

There's no call for us to finish reading this book – or any other book – if we believe that life is meaningless. What's the point in reading it if we think that the outcome will be worth nothing? Meaning is value; and when we say that there is no meaning in our existence, this implies that our value is equal to zero. And if our value is equal to zero, how can the whole of our actions be greater than the sum of our worth? When the rudder of our life lacks meaning, absurdity and haphazardness will jump in and assume control of our life. We will simply seek pleasure, and will shortcut the long routes to achievement through immoral means. Meaning contributes to setting ethical limits and creates the railroad track on which we travel towards our goals. Meaning is the basket that accommodates all the meanings of our life, and it is the thread that pulls together the "necklace" of the jewels of the meanings that encircle our lives – and that is the ultimate meaning.

If the greater meaning of our life is lacking, the lives of the majority of us will remain without a necklace that puts all meanings together, or it might turn into an impermanent pleasure, the meaning of which will not be worth more than that of a vanished pleasure.

When Meaning Retreats Diseases Advance

If we lose beloved relatives, life will continue. When we discover information that will lead to us losing our fortune, our home life will continue. But if we exclude the life meaning of our loved ones, or of our money; we still lose. Disease will advance, and life may not continue because we lack a meaning of life. Researchers found that lack of meaning in life causes emotional and behavioural disorders, many treatments developed. Viktor Frankl [3] developed a therapy that helps

---

[3] V. Frankl, Man's search for meaning, New York, NY: Simon & Schuster, 1959.

patients find meaning in their lives. Frankl regarded the lack of meaning as disastrous. Therefore, the presence of meaning in life is a most important aim. Yalom[4] also proposed a group of ideas regarding logo therapy. He mentioned that therapists need to challenge the convictions and beliefs of their patients. The efficacy of meaning of life therapy has been proven[5]. This is also what Sanders,[6] Frankl and Morita,[7] Breitbart and Henry[8] found out. Therapeutic intervention has proved to be effective and the quality of patients' lives improved by means of improving the meaning of life.

How Important Is the Meaning of Our Lives for Wellbeing?

Researchers have concluded that people who think their life has a meaning are happier. Researchers have also found that people who know the meaning of their life feel they are more fulfilled,

---

4 1 I. D. Yalom, *Existential Psychotherapy*, Basic Books, New York, NY, 1980.

5 C.J. Gelso, E. Nutt Willams & B. Fretz, Counseling Psychology, 3rd edn., American Psychological Association, Washington DC, 2014.

6 Barna Konkoly Thegeab, Adrienne Staudera and Maria S. Koppa, " 'Relationship between meaning in life and intensity of smoking: do gender differences exist?' Psychology & Health, vol. 25, no. 5, 2010.

7 V.E. Frankl, Man's search for meaning, 5th edn, tr. I. Lasch, Bacon Press, Boston, 2006 (Original work published 1946).

8 E. Mok, et al., 'The meaning of life intervention for patients with advanced-stage cancer: development and pilot study', *Oncology Nursing Forum*, vol. 39, no. 6, 2012.

and lead their lives more positively.[9] Diener[10] says that the presence of a meaning in life is linked to a positive effect on emotional wellbeing. Positive Psychology has begun to be interested in searching for the factors that lead to positivity. One of those factors is the meaning in life.[11] It is very important for our emotional wellbeing, and is no less important than the other factors, such as self-confidence [12], self-actualization and optimism.[13]

The Meaning of Life Complements our Emotional Wholesomeness

If you ask most humans about the meaning of their lives, they will not have a clear or definite answer. However, they are healthy. So, how can someone who doesn't know the meaning of their life be healthy?

---

[9] D. L. Debats, P. M. van der Lubbe, & F. R. A. Wezeman, 'On the psychometric properties of the Life Regard Index (LRI): A measure of meaningful life', Personality and Individual Differences, vol. 14, no. 2, 1993, pp. 337-345.

[10] E. Diener, 'The Science of well-being', Social Indicators Research Series, Springer Netherlands, vol. 37, 2009, pp. 11-58.

[11] J. Lyke, 'Associations among Aspects of Meaning in Life and Death Anxiety in Young Adults', Death Studies, vol. 37, no. 5, 2013, pp. 471-482. Available from CINAHL with Full Text, EBSCO host, (accessed 8 January 2017).

[12] M. F. Steger et al., 'The Meaning in Life Questionnaire: Assessing the presence of and search for meaning in life', Journal of Counseling Psychology, vol. 53, no. 1, 2006, pp. 80-93.

[13] W. C. Compton et al., 'Factor structure of mental health measures', Journal of Personality and Social Psychology, vol. 71, 1996, pp. 406-413.

Terry Eagleton answers this query in his book *The Meaning of Life*.[14] We will find that each individual has devised his own special formula, which is different from the formulas of others. This answers the query about the meaning of life. We will notice the following important aspect: that all their opinions, ways, actions, moves, expressions, ethics, ambitions and habits are concordant with the formula they have devised for themselves about the meaning of life. This is identical to Frankl's[15] theory that each person has his own meaning of life.

When we ask a person, and he doesn't give us a clear answer about the meaning of his life, this doesn't mean that his life has no meaning. He certainly knows what is important in the "formula" of his life, but the overall meaning of his life may not be clear to him. The meaning of life "contributes to explaining our everyday events, organizing them, determining what is important, setting our goals, and ranking the importance of the issues that we live", as Frankl[16] found out. But, the clarity of the meaning of life contributes to a better life. Both Chamberlain and Zika concluded that persons with a clear meaning in their

---

[14] T. Eagleton, The Meaning of Life. Translated to Arabic by Ahd Ali Deeb, Dar Al-Farqad, 2010.

[15] V. E. Frankl, The Doctor and the Soul: From psychotherapy to logo therapy, Vintage Books, New York, 1965.

[16] Ibid.

life enjoy more positivity in life.[17] So, if meanings exist in our life - whether we realize them or not - we now wonder:

What are the Meanings of Life?

Researchers' results have differed in determining what the meaning of life is. A group of researchers from several American Universities[18] have tracked the meanings of life of ten women. It was concluded that the meanings of their life are derived from their social relationships, developing themselves, and from religion and their spiritual meanings. This is different from what researcher Baumeister[19] concluded, who mentioned in the results of his research that the meaning of life depends on the presence of aims in life, achieving results, and the presence of values and self-esteem.

Researcher Emmons[20] states that the meaning of life depends on

---

[17] K. Chamberlain & S. Zika, 'Religiosity, life meaning and wellbeing: Some relationships in a sample of women', Journal for the Scientific Study of Religion, vol. 27, no. 3, 1988.

[18] C. E. Hill, 'What's it all about? A qualitative study of meaning in life for counselling psychology doctoral students', *Journal of Counselling Psychology Quarterly*, vol. 28, no. 1, 2015, pp. 1-26.

[19] R. F. Baumeister, Meanings of life, Guilford, New York, 1991.

[20] R. A. Emmons, 'Personal goals, life meaning, and virtue: Wellsprings of a positive life', in C. Keyes & J. Haidt (eds.), *Flourishing: Positive psychology and the well-lived life*, American Psychological Association, Washington, 2003, pp. 105–128.

the presence of aims and chasing after them, whereas Yalom[21] concludes that the meaning of life depends on our view of our significance in our own life. Steger,[22] as well, stressed the person's view of their significance, determining their mission in life, and their comprehensive desires. As for Csikszentmihalyi,[23] he mentioned that a person's being kind contributes to the presence of meaning in life.

Where do Meanings Come From?

Life has many meanings, these meanings are important, they add value to our life. Among those meanings, some are present meanings, and some are prospective. Some are tangible and perceptible, and some are visualized. Our sense of significance remains the ultimate sign of meaning and the source of our sense of value. That is where Steger[24] has gone ahead of us; he states that the meaning of life is in applying a sense of significance to a

---

[21] I. D. Yalom, Existential Psychology, Basic Books, New York, 1980.

[22] M. F. Steger, Meaning in life, in S. J. Lopez & C. R. Snyder (eds.), Oxford handbook of positive psychology, 2nd edn., Oxford University Press, Oxford,2009, pp. 679–687.

[23]M.Csikszentmihalyi, Flow: The psychology of optimal experience, HarperCollins, New York, 1991. [SEP]

J. Dewey, Art as Experience, Penguin, New York, 1934.

[24] Steger, op. cit. and E. Bodner, Y. S. Bergman, S. Cohen-Fridel, 'Do Attachment Styles Affect the Presence and Search for Meaning in Life', Journal of Happiness Studies, vol. 15, no. 5, 2014, pp.1041–1059.

common group of factors in life, these factors impact your feelings, aim and mission in life. For example, a person who owns rare antiques will pay a fortune for them, and give them a very high value, because he sees their significance. Whoever sees the significance in his pleasure, and regards life as perishable and evanescent, will follow his pleasure wherever it takes him. However, we all see life and its meanings differently, and we get to know them in different ways.

Among those ways are:

Money

The delicious food, the comfortable home, the fast airplane with spacious seats, and the luxury that gives us happy moments are additional meanings to the meanings of our life. Who does not see the appeal of sitting in high-ceiling halls, and the pleasure of conversing at the dinner table while being served a delicious meal, or lying down on a feather bed being massaged to sleep? Luxury presents a kind of physical pleasure within our bodies, and that is why we try to repeat and duplicate it; so, luxury in itself can easily turn into an aim.

Luxury is brought about by money. Without money, we must toil to be fed, and labour to buy accommodation. We will not need anyone to massage our feet to send us to sleep as sleep will be easy when we work so hard. Extreme fatigue will send us to sleep and our thoughts about sleep preoccupy us, but we don't get enough of it. Money brings us many of the pleasures in life, and when we begin to experience those pleasures that money can bring, we are soon convinced of the importance of having money.

It is the easiest way to make friends. We do not need to convince them that we are good enough in order for them to befriend us; our money will get the mission done. We don't need to convince our family and co-workers of our theories and convictions. Let us say whatever we want. Our theories - with some generosity - will become built upon solid foundations, and they will follow our opinions and orientations. Most people believe that money is the proof of wisdom and rationality, even if it really isn't present at all. Money also lets us be funny and have a sense of humour, it allows people to be influential; our money will carry out the mission of moderating our silly jokes.

This is where the importance of money manifests; because of its magical effect on us and on those who own it. Then, in time, we will shape our convictions using its importance, and start chasing it. The value of money for some people could rise to the level of holiness, and the life of those who hallow it becomes meaningless without it.

When we hallow money, we don't call into question our convictions of its importance. Our money might be nothing but an inheritance that we have had handed to us, or an opportunity that we have cashed in on. This could mean that we are not regarded as efficient by anyone, but the influence of money on social relationships still remains a magical one, no matter how that money has come about.

We are also in the era when money can buy what cannot be bought before. Today, tourism has become an invitation to rich people to buy pleasure. This country sells delicious food; that one sells recreational tourism and activities; yet another is filled with museums and relics. Money to travel can allow the rich to seek everything from unethical pleasures that may include sexual gratification and drugs, to beautiful natural scenes. Whoever doesn't have money may be deprived of all that.

Money also buys loyalty, and makes others unwilling to depart the circle of the luxury of our money. Money also buys prestige. For example, without money, the chances of being nominated for election would be tiny. Money brings us the invitation cards to attend congresses and exhibitions, and it is the best card with which to introduce ourselves to people. It suffices to write our prestigious titles underneath our names, to have our importance and position recognized. The theory of capitalism, that is absolutely dominant in the economies of most countries, gives money priority and dominance in many communities today.

Therefore, money presents many meanings to our life; it can buy beauty, it can buy luxury, it facilitates making friends, and many, many more amazing meanings.

A Life Partner and Children

Our spouse and children are the source of happiness for many of us. Cheerfulness sneaks in to our being just by looking at their faces, or feeling their care and communicating with them. The loving and tender spouse and the loyal child are the most beautiful roses in life's garden. Similarly, the disagreeable partner and the rebellious child are the hell of our life. Our other half gives us a basket full of various meanings, which result from the pleasure of sharing the bed; the romantic moments; the feeling that this partner is a complement to the imperfections of ourselves; and the genuine mutual care for each other, such that if one of us is hurting, the other will hurt as well. When the feelings of sincere love overwhelm us, as well as the sharing of happy moments, life will flow with its most beautiful meanings - so many sincere, genuine and enduring meanings. This is exactly what researcher Audi[25] has concluded in his research in 2005[26]; that meanings can come from the presence of an aim or a love that fills our life, or from moral standards.

However, the staircase of the meanings of marriage – although they are many – is not enough to be all the meanings of life. For the person who sees their whole life as part of a pair and nothing else, it is as if they are seeing life through a pair of glasses. So, if death takes away one of them, the death of the other will be hastened - especially for those whose togetherness has lasted for a long time. Life loses its meanings for the other partner. If the

---

[25] R. Audi, 'Intrinsic value and meaningful life', Philosophical Papers, vol. 34, no. 3, 2005, pp. 331–355.

[26] Audi as cited in Wim De Muijnck, 'The Meaning of Lives and the Meaning of Things', Journal of Happiness Studies, vol. 14, no. 4, 2013, pp. 1291–1307.

marriage was your only meaning in life, you are left with nothing.

Achievement and Productivity

Achieving goals – our achievements are proof to others of our excellence – but perhaps more importantly, they are the proof which a person provides to himself of his capabilities and capacities. When the achieved goal is big or great, it will make the meaning of his life bigger and greater. Therefore, achieving goals creates importance twice; first to ourselves, and then, it creates importance in the image that the people who surround us have of us. Therefore, when we achieve our financial, social or political goals, our self-esteem will be boosted, and we will feel that our life has clearer meanings after we achieve our goals.

This is similar to what researcher Baumeister[27] concluded; he mentioned that meanings can *be* from the existence of a goal in life, values, productivity and self-esteem. However, people who make the meaning of life restricted to achieving a goal will face a real problem after achieving that goal - like the athletes who chase "breaking the world record".

They think that importance lies in breaking someone else's record, and placing a new record themselves, and this is why they keep practicing strenuously, day in day out. However, when

---

[27] R. F. Baumeister, Meanings of life, New York, The Guilford Press, 1991.

24

they have achieved the goal that they have put all their energy into, depression can set in. The goal through which he sees life and all its meanings is now behind him. Therefore, a goal in itself is not sufficient to be a meaning of life.

Power

Dominance over others, and their submission to us and to our will, has a lustre that no one can deny; that is why killing, assault and torture play a big part in history.

That is why history tells us its ugliest stories about how a son killed his father to rule instead of him; or banished him to gain absolute authority instead of him. For power, nations have fought, the ancient and modern kingdoms wrestled, and the people of politics are still forming parties in order to have the greater power. For the sake of power, political deals are made, consciences are bought and morals are sold.

The hallowing and aggrandizement of people of high rank often shows its face in meetings and formal occasions, reinforcing the meaning of power and its high value. Titles are added and names of power brokers are omitted; they are called 'His Excellency the Minister' or 'His Majesty the King'. This is what makes the people of prominent position adore their positions which make them almost saintly and grand in the eyes of other people. Their decisions could give glory and importance to themselves and also to others. Just by signing an appointment letter, a person can be transformed from obscurity to a person of high rank, surrounded by the media with their microphones, eager to pick up his words and whispers.

This is what Frankl [28] concluded. He also mentioned that pleasure and power are not meanings of life. Frankl asserted that the meaning of life is in productivity and success, in kindness, honesty and beauty.

Friends

Friends are a need that we cannot dispense with when it comes to sharing our concerns and the difficulties of our lives. We need people to whom we can reveal our life secrets, so that they can see the full picture and give us their advice about our lives. Without this revelation, we will not get an opinion that matches our situation. And just like we reveal our imperfections to them, they will reveal theirs to us.

Our need for honest communication is common, and an external view of our life will help us with our choices, and help us to determine the direction of our decisions.

Although we reveal a lot of our flaws to our friends, this revelation makes our feeling about their sharing free from artificiality, and makes the pleasure of sharing soar into the sky without a roof. I have talked about this in my book *5 Essential*

---

[28] V. Frankl, Man's Search for Meaning, New York, NY, Simon & Schuster, 1959.

Dimensions, in the chapter on 'Social Equilibrium'; about our need to surround ourselves with people who love us from the bottom of their hearts. This is how life gets collared with its most beautiful meanings.

Hobbies, Sciences and Technology

Engaging in our hobbies makes us lose track of time and place. Some are keen on music and others on reading. There are so many hobbies; gardening has its own pleasure, as well as the many different types of sport, keeping pets, collecting possessions, travelling, journeys and adventures. We may find out that hobbies come close to being an addiction. This is generally a harmless addiction, but some people do find that they become truly addicted to their hobby and obsessed with it.

Hobbies endow our lives with meanings. Hobbyists gather together and converse for hours about the tiniest details without getting bored. They long to meet up even more often; to speak with others that share this common meaning. They desire for the meanings that are brought about by their hobbies to stay with them for longer.

Some hobbies are practiced in the area of technology, such as those related to cars or motorbikes, video games and computers. No one living in this century is ignorant of the numerous and countless meanings provided by science and technology, which make us immerse ourselves in them completely. Technology has produced the devices that connect us to what is so far away. It has produced airplanes that soar with us above the clouds. It also produced telescopes that show us deep into the vast universe; and the development of musical instruments that play the most marvellous of tunes.

It also produced the cooking tools that delight us with preparing the tastiest, great-looking and quick-cooking delicacies. Thus, we are not astonished that science and technology present a meaning that beautifies our life and ornaments it. When we lose our cell-phones, we lose dozens of meanings that this phone provides us with, which enhance and beautify our life.

The same applies to art, which artists dive into, and spend their days amidst their paintings, or with their musical instruments. So are the hobbies that rob the lives of those obsessed with them for many years - be they hunters, mountain climbers or rare antique collectors. There remains for us to know that those who lived before us didn't have as many hobbies, and weren't enchanted by technology.

Flanagan[29] agrees with us that science, technology, principles and politics provide us with a meaning in life.

---

[29] O. Flanagan, The Really Hard Problem: Meaning in a material world, MIT Press, Cambridge, MA, 2007.

Human Meanings

The noble meanings of stretching a helping hand to others, and taking care of them, might be the shortest route to fulfilment. Having a positive impact on the lives of others provides our life with a noble meaning that outstrips all the other modest meanings that come about through taking or through diligence.

Persistent giving is the nobler meaning that feeds our contentment and inner fulfilment more rapidly and concisely - just as Kim[30] concluded. Kim mentioned that volunteer work leads to immense contentment and fulfilment.

Life is a Basket Full of Meanings

The meanings we have reviewed are the most common ones, but of course there are many others; for life is a basket full of meanings that cannot pass out of our sight. Even during our suffering, we discover new meanings in our life, having the flavour of suffering. Even for him to whom the meaning and meanings of life have vanished, still their disappearance does mean that they never existed.

The causes of this disappearance are numerous; there might be an agonizing affliction, such as pain, during which we are unable to think of anything else. When we lose someone that we have

---

[30] A. E. Kim, 'Religious influences on personal and societal wellbeing', Social Indicators Research, vol. 62, no. 1-3, 2003, pp. 149– 170.

become so attached to, the system of our life and its meaning fall apart because we have set this person as one of the supporting pillars to the meaning of our life.

The disappearance of meaning from our field of vision cannot mean its absence from all fields of vision. The meaning of life is like the taste of food. A toothache, an oral infection, a fever, or any other cause, could impair our ability to taste. However, if the taste of food vanishes from our mouths, our companions sharing the same meal with us will still be able to taste it. Those who taste food, without any hindrances blocking its deliciousness, will find that the meal tastes good, even if we cannot.

The same applies to life; life is a meal rich in meanings, and these meanings encircle the life of every living being, whether the latter tasted it or not. Even if some of us lose sight of it, due to a financial difficulty, an emotional disturbance that impairs our ability to see any beauty, or due to the disappearance of these meanings temporarily, because of, for example, the death of a beloved one, life will remain a basket full of meanings.

We ought to find and recognize the basket just as we have got to know its constituents. We ought to wonder why all these meanings exist in our life. It could be that these meanings are the reason for us to identify the cause of our being alive, or they may have guided us to know the ultimate meaning that lies behind these meanings.

The meaning of life is no new topic for human beings; there

have been multiple past attempts to discover the meaning of life. In the past, philosophers have sought to answer that question. Religions, too, have provided other answers to the very same question. In modern times, science has given marvellous answers about the beginning of the universe and the evolution of life. After science had been promoted to that rank, some scientists attempted to give an answer about the meaning of our being alive.

Since we are seeking the complete truth, we will review together some of the conclusions drawn by each of these three parties. Afterwards, we will return to our question about the presence of these meanings in our lives.

Chapter 2

The Meaning of Life from the Perspective of Science

The Chess Board

Once upon a time, a genius made a chess game for an emperor. It was said that he created a strategic game. For a player to win, he needed to foresee the steps and moves of his opponent and plan ahead. This game was played on a wooden board with 64 squares, with different stones. Each of them had an individualized move. There was a king, queen, pawns, rooks, knights and bishops. The player who would knock down the other player's king would win the game.

The maker of this game was brilliant in both the innovation of it, and also in choosing the reward the emperor would bestow on him. When the emperor told him, "Name your reward," the game maker replied by asking the emperor for a doubling grain of wheat. The emperor wondered, "In what way should the grain be doubling?" The game maker answered, saying that he desired a grain of wheat to be placed on the first square of the chess board, two grains on the second square, four grains on the third, eight on the fourth, and so on until all the squares were filled. After having bidden the vizier entrusted to the emperor's storehouses to grant the game-maker this gift, the emperor then realized his mistake. The greatest storehouses of the emperor did not suffice to fill all sixty-four squares!

This story is an analogy that draws us a picture of how far humanity has progressed in terms of knowledge. Science has started so tiny, like the single grain of wheat on the first square. We used to ignite fire by striking stones together. We used to make trinkets by heating them until they fused. A little bit of science has accompanied us through many long centuries, though it is not clear that it can continue to move along in its progress indefinitely.

Nevertheless, through the past few centuries, we have succeeded at multiplying our science stores, and we've moved swiftly along the board of science. We have landed robots on Mars, discovered our gene map and unravelled so many of the mysteries of the universe. That which is far away seems all the closer. We've overcome so many difficulties: we can make hot places cooler and cold places warmer, we've mastered fashion design, beautified faces, conquered some diseases, and enjoyed daydreaming through watching movies.

Science is the future that awaits humanity. Science matters significantly to us today, and this is why we search for the meaning of life amongst the pages of science books, and amongst scientists' most famous quotes. Will the steady increase of knowledge in the sciences guide us to recognizing the meaning of our life?

The Meaning of Life from the Scientific Perspective

It seems to me that there is no branch in experimental sciences that searches into the meaning of life. However, some scientists' efforts will be examined for relevance to the hunt for the meaning of life. This section will Biology and address the Theory of Evolution; the work of Richard Dawkins will be discussed. This section will also look at Astronomy and the work of Stephen Hawking, amongst others.

The Perspective of Biology and the Theory of Evolution

Biology – for anyone who isn't too familiar with it – is one of the sciences that has made rapid leaps in the field of science and learning, and is an ancient science. Biology studies life, including human life. Biologists' believe our earliest pre-human ancestors engaged in a sort of proto-biology, determining which species we could eat, and which species could kill us, and they studied the natural world as a practical means of survival. With Darwin's powerful explanatory theory of evolution through natural selection, confirmed with every new advance, from genetics 100 years ago through to modern genomics, we now know how living organisms have evolved and how they adapt to their surrounding environment. We know how our living cells function, how our genes affect us, and how genetic factors in particular determine the predisposing factors to hereditary diseases, or even to personality traits.

We can now see the mechanism of development of living organisms, and we are able to identify the creatures that are closest to us, and have physical similarities to our own bodies. Experiments on those creatures have provided us with a lot of information, through which we can live longer, healthier lives. We don't know where science will take us in this regard, with some scientists proposing that we are on the verge of doubling or tripling human life expectancy in the near future.

Our gene map has been completed. Like finding a treasure map, we now know the genes responsible for disease and how they are inherited. However, finding the map doesn't mean we have found the treasure. Most of our diseases are still conquerors, not conquered. We have scored some goals in the net of diseases, but we haven't won yet. The game between humanity and diseases is still on.

Edward Wilson, the scientist and Pulitzer prizewinning author of dozens of scientific books and works in the fields of Biology and Biodiversity, has tried to express his stance on the meaning of life from the perspective of science. The meaning of life has always posed a difficult problem for scientists, because it falls outside the realm of testable hypotheses. We can, for example, examine what makes us happy, but that assumes that happiness is the meaning of life. Meaningfulness itself cannot be the subject of any experiment.

Biologists tend to see all life as a continuum. From the earthworm to the eagle, all creatures share certain characteristics and are evolved from a common ancestor. Humans are advanced apes in the scientific view, and there is absolutely no doubt about this fact in terms of evidence. Perhaps surprisingly, then, Wilson's book, *"The Meaning of Human Existence"*,[31] takes a radical stance, saying that humans really are distinct from other animals. From the art we create, to our understanding of our past, and our abilities to shape the future, humans are more than simply hyper-intelligent apes. These differences make us something other than just animals. To Wilson, this great intelligence and the power to destroy this unique and beautiful planet upon which we live gives us great responsibilities. We are all stewards of this planet, and to Wilson, this gives us a purpose, imposed upon us by our great intellect and abilities. But a common purpose in meeting the challenges of the 21st century is not the same as a deep and permanent meaning of existence in general, any more than defeating Hitler was the meaning of life for the mid 20th century. Wilson provides a call to arms that could provide meaningful purpose, just as how helping the poor and kindness to strangers make us feel better. But common goals and purpose do not give an answer to the meaning of man's existence.

Similar scientific difficulties about the meaning of existence can be seen in a videotaped encounter between the famous biologist,

---

[31] E. O. WILSON, The Meaning of Human Existence, Liveright Publishing Corporation, New York, NY, 2014.

evolutionist and ethologist, Richard Dawkins, [32] and some students who were asking him about the meaning of life. Dawkins answered:

"What's the meaning of life? In honour on an evolutionary worldview, one thing to say is that the universe doesn't owe us any meaning. It could be that there is no meaning of life, and, if so, that would be just tough. I don't believe that to be the case, because I think that we can all make whatever meaning we choose to make, and you, each of you, will have plenty of meanings in your own life. You'll be enthusiastic about some things; maybe some sport you play, maybe some books you read, maybe your love life, maybe your family life. Maybe some of you love nature, some of you love music. These are all individual meanings that you can give to your life. That doesn't mean that life itself has one special meaning. It doesn't mean that we are here for any particular purpose any more than mountains are here for a purpose, or rocks are here for a purpose. Rocks are just here. Rocks just happened, they are simply just here. Mountains just happened, they too are just are here. There is a sense in which life is just here. Life came about through the evolutionary process, but after billions of years of evolution, life forms arose that had big brains, and complex nervous systems. We've got the biggest brains of all for our size, and so, our brains

---

[32] Richard Dawkins - Life May Be Meaningless, [online video], 2015, https://www.youtube.com/watch?v=IFG5qo7HbIM, (accessed 27 June 2017).

are capable of developing purposes of our own. We, with our big brains can think of our own purposes."

Here Dawkins articulates, with all his intelligence, his opinion on the matter. It is hard to argue that art, mathematics, and love give meaning to people in diverse ways. To Dawkins, an avowed atheist, we simply are here, with our big brains, and those brains are capable of searching for meaningful things to do that make us feel as if we have a purpose. But just as art, science, love or saving the Earth from environmental catastrophe can be meaningful, feeling good about ourselves is not enough to fill in the meaning of life in general. Dawkins himself acknowledges this in his answer's first lines: "from a purely evolutionary point of view, the universe doesn't owe us a meaning".

Before that encounter, Richard Dawkins released his documentary with the title *Sex, Death and The Meaning of Life*, in which he questioned the meaning of life and the purpose of our being alive. He pointed out that the meaning of life is to be kind to ourselves and to others, because that kindness is inherently found in our genes. However, he did not give an answer as to the meaning of our being alive.

In that same documentary, Dawkins interviewed an atheist. A part of the discussion was about the meaning of life. That atheist's answer was: 'to enjoy life'. After the encounter and the documentary, the question 'What is the meaning of life?' still remains unanswered.

Part of the meaning of life may include the drive to kindness that humans feel, but meeting this impulse does not fill the needed meaning of life. It was clearly evident that Dawkins had figured out an idea of a meaning of life, after it "hadn't existed", like he told those students. In the first instance, it was obvious that his ignorance regarding the existence of a meaning of life did not mean that the meaning of life does not exist; he simply didn't know it. The second time - when he said the meaning of life is to be kind- was a scientist's talk but not science's talk.[33] Moreover, the question 'What is the meaning of our existence?' cannot be answered by 'To enjoy!' Enjoyment in itself is not meaningful in the right way, because it refers to only one quality of an existence, not to the existence itself. Enjoyment is an answer to another question; 'We are now alive. What should we do?' Here, the answer 'To enjoy' is possible, but it also falls short of providing a purpose or aim to our lives, and it is definitely a scientist's answer, not a scientific answer.[34]

The Perspective of Astronomers

Astronomers – for whoever is unfamiliar with them – used to depend on their telescopes to explore the vast universe. As in biology, astronomy had a deep importance for our early

---

[33] J. C. Lennox, John C. Lennox quotes, [website], https://www.goodreads.com/author/quotes/1044434 (accessed 20 July 2017).
[34] Ibid.

ancestors, who needed to understand the seasons in order to predict when to plant their crops. Astronomy started from an understanding about the start of winter and the start of summer, the rising and setting of the sun, and the appearance of stars in the heavens. Today, with the help of physicists, they use other kinds of technologies to pick up miniscule waves that can tell more about the extent of the universe, which goes beyond the work of telescopes. They have realized the size of the universe, and its age, with proof and evidence, and they have ascertained in an undoubted manner that the universe is expanding.

The most famous contemporary astronomer and physicist, Professor Stephen Hawking, conducted a great deal of valuable research in his field, and endeavoured to answer the question about the meaning of life in the documentary *The Meaning of Life*[35]. The answer was that there is nothing in life but physics: no matter how it seems to common sense, everything in human experience and existence in general is the interplay of fundamental particles. The laws of physics allow the emergence of consciousness, which in turn creates a three-dimensional model of the outside world – a best-fit model that we call 'reality.' And the meaning of life is nothing but a piece of the

---

[35] Stephen Hawking's Grand Design. The Meaning of Life [online video], 2015, https://www.youtube.com/watch?v=9eD64HzP3yQ, (accessed 20 February 2018).

model of reality that we each build inside our own brain. The meaning of life is what we choose it to be.

Perhaps this suggests to Professor Hawking that life, when understood from this perspective, has no meaning in a broader sense?

We have heard the views of great and intelligent scientists, grappling with the meaning of life.

However, the tools of science are very specific, and limited. Just as an accountant follows rules for accounting, a scientist is constrained by the rules of science. Questions like "What is the meaning of life?" cannot be scientifically addressed. The late evolutionary biologist, and influential spokesperson for science, Stephen J. Gould, considered that science and religion were distinct and non-overlapping "magisteria", two separate kingdoms or domains, like England and France with their water border in-between. He supported the idea that science could address matters that can be addressed by experimentation, but that spiritual matters could not be scientifically addressed. The matters of spirituality must be taken up on their own terms.

Conclusion

It is clear that Wilson, Dawkins and Hawking are intelligent, well-read and thoughtful people. But the fact that they are scientists does not mean that their opinions are pure scientific thinking. Every scientist will also hold their own opinions and biases.

Even though the above scientists appeared to be writing or speaking on the meaning of life and its determination, none of them actually gave a clue as to "the meaning of life". Sometimes publishers and television producers will push a title upon a scientist, in order to sell more books or to gain a wider audience. The scientist may object, but in the end agree with the over-extending title, because like most people, they want their opinions to be heard. It is likely that none of these scientists truly believed that they had discovered the meaning of life. Dawkins and Hawking believe that there is none, but these are untestable opinions. Wilson and Gould believe that there is purpose in life, and like Dawkins and Hawking, find meaningful ways with which to spend their time, but again, these are not the conclusions of experimental science, but rather, the philosophical musings of thoughtful and intelligent people. It is clearly evident that science has no answers to these kinds of questions, and most of science makes no attempt to answer inquiries as to the meaning of life, any more than accountants try to create art using only the tools of accounting.

The scientific inability to answer drives us to move on to the logical questions that result from the absence of an answer to the meaning of life. If there is no scientific meaning of life, why then do we need a meaning to be emotionally healthy? What is the point of being alive if life has no meanings? What is the reason behind our ability to reason? If being alive is meaningless, why then do we produce great art? Why do we have all our maturity and awareness?

Why do we search for meanings? Should we create life meanings that suit us? What is the meaning of life that could be suitable for an old man? Is it feeding his dog and looking after his pets? Gather up all those meanings that encircle our life? Are there any good reasons?

Scientists cannot give answers to the question 'What is the meaning of life?', and for the most part, following Gould's split between scientific and religious magisteria,[36] they do not even try. It is simply outside their discipline. This does not mean we should dismiss science as weak. Science has brought us to great understanding of the natural and physical world. Science has extended our lives, and given us the free time to ponder and enjoy life. Science has brought us the modern world, and to reject science is to long for a return to the darkest days of humanity, full of disease, misery, and superstition. However, when scientists ponder the meaning of life, they do so outside the rules of their discipline. We may choose to listen to their words, and some may find comfort and meaning in them. But they are only the opinions of scientists, practicing outside their discipline, just as a famous celebrity may use her fame to advocate for hunger-relief.

---

[36] Stephen Jay Gould. The Evolution of Life on Earth.
http://www.blc.arizona.edu/courses/schaffer/449/Gould%20Nonoverlapping%20Magis teria.htm (accessed 08/11/2017).

Why Science Does Not Give a Meaning of Life

In this section, I will clarify why the meaning of life is lacking among the folds of science. What makes me do that? It can seem a mistake or an ugly truth to attempt to criticize our attachment to science; but such is necessary because science, which has dramatically altered our way of handling our life events, and which provides solid evidence about historical facts, fails to give an answer about the meaning of our life.

In the contemporary world, science is like the star of a movie, who appears all through our moments on the "stage" of our life. Nonetheless, he disappears from the most important scene of all—"the meaning of life". Many of us are emotionally attached to science. We would like science to have the final word on all questions, including defining the meaning of life. However, science remains silent, and cannot get the final word on defining the meaning of our life. We come across some scientists that misuse this emotional attachment in order to uphold their fame. They give people what they want to hear: that the meaning of life can be determined by science – which isn't true.

Science (today) has nothing to say about the meaning of life; but this may change in the future, and at some point science may have the answer. The reasons that prevent science from contributing to defining the meaning of life currently are as follows:

If we divide the life which humans live, into circles, it would be like an egg, consisting of albumen (egg white), yolk and shell.

Science, though, is only additive; it does not change the basic constituent composition of the egg of life.

The Yolk of the Egg of Our Life

We will find the yolk of the egg is our "life and death", which has not changed since our first ancestors, and is something science will not touch. Life will remain life, and he who is dead will remain dead whether we reach Mars or invade the nearby galaxies. If science cures all diseases, the dead will remain in their death, and the living will die, and science will never manage to bring the dead to life or prevent the living from dying.

The Albumen of the Egg of our Life

Within the albumen of the egg of our life exist matters which do not change. Within all human beings whether they are rich or poor, and among human beings who ever lived in the past or are living today or will live in the future, within them all exist the stages of our life. Childhood will remain childhood with all its weakness and ignorance, and youth will remain youth with all its excitement, energy and changes that happen to the body. Maturity and old age did not and will not change as well. Within the albumen of the egg of our life, you will find our motives and instincts that have not and will not change; money, influence, happiness, the desire to have children, desire for rest, and desire for beauty. All of mankind's oldest motives are exactly the same as our motives today. We will also find in that circle our needs that do not change, the need for shelter, drink and food, and those needs will never stop. We can think of these as both basic to human life and as instinctual.

The Shell of the Egg of Our Life

The poor starve and the rich starve, the first man also starved, but we do not eat equally. This person eats more, and that person eats less. Some eat better, and others do not eat healthily, yet we all feel full. One may drink from the mire, while another drinks avocado juice with honey, therefore we differ in the fulfilment of our desires in hunger and thirst. The shell of the egg of life is the changeable contingencies of human existence. These can be found in food and drink as well as in clothing, housing and adornment, and that is what science could change. Humans, a thousand years ago, were suffering from the cold, but today are more prepared with equipment designed for heating. They were also suffering from heat, but technology made many of the warm places moderate because of air-conditioning, and all that because of science. It is science that made our clothes perfect, beautified our faces with beauty products, eradicated some diseases, made us enjoy dreams while we are awake when we watch movies and is the future that awaits human kind. But all that science offers does not exceed the shell of the egg of our life.

How Can the Vast Difference Between Human Beings be Just Shells?

The difference between the rich and the poor is the difference between a man who lived 1000 years ago and the man who lives today. The difference touches the ends of our lives, the ancient man gets ill and we get ill, many of today's poor still do not get treatment. Many people today still do not know what life can be about, other than work and making an effort without rest. They do not take airplanes, do not carry smart phones, grand cooking equipment does not grace their kitchens, and everything that science came up with is irrelevant to them. But yet they live, reproduce and pass on to each other their cultural heritage and live with us on the same planet. They have not become extinct, and still their lives, as those of the past, have meanings.

Science has overcome many diseases, and found various solutions to the remaining diseases, while yet more are still being studied. It is science that brought us airplanes and cars and what is to come will be even greater, but the truth remains, that the core or yolk of our lives will not be changed by the car we ride, and will not change if the train goes slowly or passes us like a lightning bolt. The core of our lives will not change because of the class of seat we are in. The passengers will remain having the premonitions that the plane may crash—if an engine burns— whether they are in first class or economy class, people will remain people, even if the number of zeros of their bank accounts exceeds our ability to count. Death awaits at the end of the road, and life remains between its yolk and albumen without change. Our love for wives and children, and the desire for influence and achievements, all those things are outside the circle of science, and science cannot change their core being. If science colours the shell of our egg with the most beautiful colours, death with its dark colour will remain our end, and life will remain with its phases and stages, and man will remain man with his motives and desires.

Ignorance Achieves Goals More Than Science

In 2006, the Nobel Prize in Physics was awarded to two scientists who were able to contribute to the discovery of the Big Bang Theory (the Great Explosion Theory of how the universe began). They came up with scientific evidence about two questions:

How did the universe start? And when did it start? They provided evidence for the expansion of the universe, waves that prove that an explosion happened and other evidence. However, within that information, there is a set of questions that remain without answers, we still do not know the source of the materials that exploded in that Big Bang (great explosion), and we do not know the cause of that explosion. The more science reveals on its answer sheet, ignorance reveals to us yet more sheets of questions.

Science reveals simultaneously both knowledge and ignorance together as a general base not only for physics, but for all sciences. Every scientific research starts with a question or two to which the researcher is trying to find an answer. He could end up finding answers for those questions or end up not being able to answer them at all, but in all cases these answers will produce a further set of questions which the researcher leaves to future researchers to come along and find answers to.

As we have shown at the beginning of the book, the meaning of our lives has been proven by researchers, and that the meaning of life is the overall meaning of all existence. If science works in

49

such a way that it provides one answer and at the same time brings forth a set of questions, then the final result of the match between science and ignorance would not be the dominance of science. With each question solved, even more are created. It is true that science has scored many goals against ignorance, however, ignorance remains the side which has the most goals, and that is on the general level for "team science and team ignorance", and on the "league" match level, in the field of "the meaning of life", it seems that team science is unable to score scientific goals when it comes to the meaning of life; the researchers and most successful studies of "the reason for our existence" did not provide scientific answers to that question.

Science Eases and Hardens Life

The results of scientific researches and experiments have not sat idly in the laboratory. The results of science have invaded our lives, and have impacted the way we think and our way of life. Every field that science touched, we find that it was directly introduced for the purpose of easing our lives, yet it also created new burdens for us. These burdens are indirect, but have consequences for us, because of it, life in other aspects becomes harder indirectly.

Following are some examples of this.

Science and Work

In the past, scientists travelled to far lands to gain knowledge, and there was not much in the way of science, but today, the lives of scientists and specialists have become easier in many ways. Universities are filled with specializations. Today however, gaining academic certificates has become extremely difficult due to the sheer amount of knowledge that exists today that students are required to be familiar with before graduating. As the academic assignments given to the students have become exhausting, where a student has to spend most of his/ her daily hours in reading research papers, and today those who graduate are required to pass employment tests in prestigious and desirable places, it all becomes extremely complicated. And finding fulfilling employment requires a miracle, and maintaining it after we have found it requires dedication, the result being that science has created many job opportunities, but has also made it difficult in other ways.

With regards to gaining knowledge after studies, it has become easier than before. In the past, specialists in Chemistry, Physics and other scientific fields were suffering from a lack of people who were able to discuss ideas about these topics. Today, because of the technological and institutional structure of science, all that has ended. Scientists today gather, discuss and view the work of their colleagues, and those who are not able to join them listen to their discussions via the internet, but the scope of the information which a specialist is required to follow will take more of his time due to its volume; such as Open Data, Knowledge Transfer programs and collaborative working. When a person is a doctor and does not follow the latest developments in his field, then his lack of follow-ups will put him in a disadvantaged position. Therefore, today's specialist will be in an awkward position, either he buries himself in pursuing science which will take up most of his time, or fall short with regards to his patients' service, who deserve to be served better.

These sciences which we are exposed to on a daily basis are becoming an additional burden on our busy and limited minds. Who could absorb all these sciences?! And a doctor, although brilliant and cautious, coming to know about all the new medicines will make him never abandon his study chair, he will continue to learn and pursue the developments in medicine, learning about harmful medicine, and the latest discoveries in science and his specialization fields. If he does all that, his life would be like the life of students on the night of the final exam, endlessly studying, and if he does not do all that, he will put people's lives in danger or prescribe unknowingly a medicine which has better alternatives or end up telling his patients that there is no cure for their disease when one has been recently developed.

The scientific development in medicine has achieved many results in understanding our bodies, diseases and dealing with them. The pain that used to make people before us scream all night is now cured with a small capsule, as a capsule also became a cure for many other diseases. The same science is what revealed to us many of today's diseases, and we became concerned about the many warnings regarding food, drink, chemotherapy or misdiagnosis.

Food was very limited in the past, when the majority of human food did not exceed two or three varieties; for example, Europeans would eat a lot of wheat or potato in the winter months, and Arabs would eat milk and dates. Food, however,[38] is now available in large quantities, and with many flavours, and this was something not even Kings and Emperors enjoyed in the past. We have them now because science enabled us to have them. Our desire for foods resulted in these foods becoming available on store shelves that do not close its doors to a buyer, selling it at the most inexpensive prices and in restaurants at reasonable prices, but collectively it is the source of diseases, due to flavourings, additives, colourings, and genetically modified food. These are the trade-offs of a scientific approach to human culture.

Our Social Lives

Consider the phone that brought the distant closer and placed our entire office in our pockets. All of us see the greatness of this achievement and its value, but many of us do not see the enormity of what it takes from us. It takes our lives from us, many unimportant matters take up the time we should be spending with our children. We follow the falls and slips of celebrities, we read people's comments about such insignificant matters. Additionally, we cannot escape unimportant messages from friends, or receiving news that has no relevance to us.

The applications of science provided us with this information but took from us our time, and life is nothing but hours that we live and then it ends. When we grow older and our duties grow with us, telephone calls that we receive become a burden which prevent us from achieving our goals. Here is a caller, speaking to us while we are busy, and here is a problem that is valid and needs time to be addressed but we have no time for it. Here is a friend with plenty of time calling in our busiest time, and so on. We cannot ignore him, and we cannot attend to his needs. Do we see these burdens as we see the benefits?

Education

Education is one aspect of life which was simpler before science entered our lives. A hundred years ago life was less noisy than today. The access our children have to all that is available from the sciences, the means of communication and the ease of getting in touch has made teaching our children more difficult; whilst in the past before science entered in our lives, if we left our child with the neighbours' children, we would often achieve the same moral standards that we wish for him. Now there are chat applications and socializing programs on our children's phones, but they remain without social skills, and we need to teach them how to interact with others, discuss, be kind, ignore and forgive, etc. Did science facilitate or complicate our social life?

These are only examples, and I put them forward to prove that science eases and at the same time hardens life. Or perhaps it does not harden or ease life; life remains life and everything that science provides only touches the shells of our lives. Perhaps life did not become complex or harder because of science, but remained as it was, and there is a direct ease and indirect hardening, and the illusion that many of us have is that science has simplified our lives and made them easier, simpler and less complicated. What science gives us directly, it takes back indirectly.

After all that is mentioned, it becomes clear that science does not touch the yolk of our life's egg or its albumen, as the core of life remains as well as death, and also the basic needs and instincts all continue unabated. The answers provided by science create new questions, and the light that science brings to brighten our lives, it brightens indeed. However, it brightens for us the windows from which we do not know what might jump. The road where we take a step forward, and then a step back, is a road that will not take us to the meaning of life.

Science is a Means and Not the Staff of Moses

Science looks for the gaps in knowledge in order to obliterate them. However, not every knowledge gap can be obliterated by science. Science fails to answer a multitude of questions. Science can neither explain the magnificence of a sonata, nor can it give an opinion on assisted suicide.[37] Science might tell us about the benefits of sleep, but does not inform us of the reason for sleep. It tells us how to arrive somewhere fast, but doesn't

---

[37] "Science has limits: A few things that science does not do",
Understanding Science, University of California Museum of Paleontology, [website],
http://undsci.berkeley.edu/article/0_0_0/whatisscience_12 (accessed 7 July 2017).

tell us *why* we are heading there. The same applies to the meaning of our life; the meaning of our life is related to the reason for our existence, and science will not tell us why we exist!

When a murderer commits murder and leaves some clues behind, forensic scientists start collecting crime scene evidence, such as a hair strand from the murderer, or a genetic fingerprint. But the murderer's hair strand will not speak out in the laboratory and say, "I belong to the murderer." Scientific research cannot provide evidence that the hair strand belongs to a person who committed murder. Therefore, the information provided by scientific research is processed using the laws of logic, which question the reason for the presence of this strand of hair, and the reason why the person to whom it belongs came into that place. The hair strand might belong to a television reporter who was on a live broadcast, and so would have been seen committing a crime. Thereby, he is excluded, disregarding the fact that scientific investigation has provided the scientific evidence. Therefore, the investigation about the murderer's identity is restarted, or the sample is re-analyzed after excluding some of the suspects.

All scientific research papers end with a discussion. When it comes to discussing the reason for our being alive, we use logic to discuss the reason for our being alive. When we do not find in scientific research what could be discussed in order to understand the meaning of life, we ought to redirect our search. Science is a means through which we reach for what we wish for. When we do not reach what we wish for, we then ought to use what will get us to our goals, and not stick to science. Science is not the staff of Moses that can do all things. When we insist on discussing the meaning of life in terms of science, but without any scientific evidence, we will end up straying away from objectivity by presenting groundless or inconsistent answers.

How Should We Approach Science, Then?

Many people do not like science and attempt to avoid owning technological devices. Some of them haven't heard yet about the Big Bang. If any of them ever gave their ear to it, they would be listening without interest. If he ever became interested, his aim would be to refute it, or to question the validity of evidence that it has been built upon. His simple life, for example, that he spends on his farm or in his rural house is all that matters to him. When he gets into his car, he is fine with just listening to the radio. His relatives have advised him, but to no avail. He doesn't feel comfortable using a sat-nav to determine his destination. He is fine with the road signs, and if he gets lost, he would ask passers-by to guide him. If he wants to travel quite a distance to another city that is four hundred kilometres away, he will play his favourite songs or tracks, and start his car engine. After a hundred kilometres, traffic backs up, and he waits until the cars start moving once more. Then traffic backs up again, cars start moving again, and traffic backs up a third time. The driver arrives at his destination after eight hours, whereas the journey should have taken three and a half hours. Will this person be equivalent to another one who found out that the traffic was congested, and chose another route, and by doing this, arrived in much less time?

We cannot put science aside; the losses would be massive, just like the losses of the driver who ignored technology, while the only thing he gained out of neglecting it was to reinforce delusions about the journey's difficulty and complexity. The same applies to neglecting science in all aspects of life; the significance of science cannot be the point of the discussion. The point is: there definitely are areas where science should be used. However, we shouldn't waste our time trying to find out road conditions and traffic jams, or any other navigation updates on the sat-nav, if we haven't determined our destination yet.

Can a Jeweller's Loupe Show us the Stars?

If we use the "spectacles" of scientific research to search for the meaning of life, we will discover that what we see cannot provide us with a meaning in life. This does not mean that the spectacles of science are worthless; it is just that it would be like someone looking at the stars through the loupe of a jeweller who sells precious stones. The jeweller's loupe is no good for viewing planets, even if it is useful for other things, such as looking at the intricacies of very small gemstones. We won't put to question the science that encircles our lives, claiming that it is futile; for science shall remain valuable, but we shall cast doubt on the ways in which some people attempt to use science.

The results of science about the meaning of our life are not correct. The collective meanings of our lives cannot be of any less importance than its meanings that we touch every day. Our money, children and relationships with our loved ones are meanings that illuminate our lives. The overall meaning of our lives must be of greater value. How can some scientists say that the meaning of our lives is our being gene dispensers; that there is no meaning for our being alive; that we are like rocks, and that the whole of our lives' meanings, which we see and feel, are equal to nothing? And how can our money, children and loved ones have a distinct meaning, while the meaning proposed by some scientists is vague and nearly empty, e.g. "to be kind"? There certainly is something wrong.

The science which we benefit from in most aspects of our life is of no use here. We ought not to conclude that science is not right; these are the efforts of scientists, and not research results. It isn't right, either, to say that our life is meaningless. This is an incorrect conclusion. Meanings encircle our lives, and we have to give discussion and logic a better chance, just as we would do when we start searching for another murderer, because the evidence negates logic.

Why is Science Silent and "Few" Scientists Speak?

Science does not provide answers to the question of the meaning of life, and the reasons that I have mentioned have prevented reaching any results. The door of science is still open to contribute; however, the previous reasons obstruct science from reaching an answer to the meaning of life, and there are other reasons that might have eluded me. For science to reach an answer is a possibility, science might be able to overcome some of these obstacles with new scientific tools, however, sciences are still silent and its silence does not mean lack of its ability to speak and it is very possible that science will speak one day. (After all, there are many topics that were once beyond science's scope that are now comfortably within; imagine considering the inner workings of cells before the invention of the microscope). In light of all that we have mentioned, we wonder: scientists speak about the meaning of life, but science is silent, therefore, how can they find ears that can listen to them? On what basis do these scientists speak?

Here are a set of reasons that help some scientists to speak while science is silent:

Showmanship

In a moment of clarity, a travel agent told me that all the money they got in the office was dirty money, and so of course, I asked him why. He told me that their sales are done in ways that attract customers based on fraud and lies, and that they publish an advertisement in the newspaper that there are a limited number of seats to travel to one of the beautiful islands, and a famous 5-star hotel at a very low price. After the advertisement is placed in the newspaper, they make the office's telephones seem busy for two hours. Afterwards they start accepting calls to tell the callers that the seats have been fully sold, and then they sell their flights at their usual price as during the rest of the week. He told me that this method of marketing is known to many business owners and they are well aware that this is a dirty marketing process, attracting customers with tempting offers that don't actually exist.

Some scientists hunt for fame with the taste of science and knowledge, and so the scientist raises the curiosity of readers that science has an answer to the meaning of life when the truth is otherwise. At the beginning of this book I talked about my journey in writing for the newspapers and wrote that the easiest way to fame is to curse celebrities (I have never done that and will never do so) but that recipe is a successful recipe which many writers know about, and that recipe is also successful in the world of books. If you wrote a book about observations and flaws of the "relativity theory" and called the book "Criticism of the Relativity Theory", be assured that your sales will not be as great as making your book title "The Stupidity of Einstein" or "The Stupid Man" and place his picture on the cover, and so it is with scientists. If they wrote about their specialties, their sales would be normal, but the books with enormous sales, you will find titled with insults to the one who is glorified by many humans...God.

Christopher Hitchens has written many books, but his book "God is not Great" within a week became the bestseller on

Amazon, up there with the sales of the famous stories of *Harry Potter*.[38]

The best investment for a well-known scientist is a book which sells millions of copies, and making that possible by naming your book *The God Delusion*, as Richard Dawkins did, where he sells millions of copies of the book annually using the same style. He could have named the book "On the Hypothesis of God's Existence," as this is the topic of the book. With even the most disciplined and objective scientists, we find that the titles of their books curve away a bit from objectivity. We have mentioned that Wilson's book *The Meaning for Human Existence*[39] did not provide an answer to the meaning of human existence. It is well known what the publishing houses do, as they are concerned with marketing standards that help the selling of the largest number of books possible and to draw attention to them, those marketing standards may conflict with scientific objectivity and ethical standards.

---

[38] Wikipedia contributors, God is not Great, *Wikipedia, The Free Encyclopedia*, [website], 2017, https://en.wikipedia.org/w/index.php?title=God_Is_Not_Great&oldid=811488443, (accessed 15 September 2017).

[39] E. O. Wilson. *The Meaning of Human Existence*, Liveright Publishing Corporation, a division of W.W. Norton, 2014.

The Simplicity of Science and the Complexity of Others

Science gives us the logical interlink, provides us with evidence that can be reassured and retested, and gives us constant relationships between things. These relationships can be of benefit to different aspects of life. When scientists added chemicals to glass and heated it, the hardness of the glass increased and produced what is known as Tempered Glass. These processes that have ended with increased glass hardness are scientific experiments that can be tested, investigated and used in different applications. We find it in car windshields and mobile phone screens, and there are many uses for this glass that confirms that relationship and so, as with all the scientific experiment results, it ends with results that make interlinks confirmed and inevitable. Whereas the information we receive from philosophers or religious scholars is not that clear and easy to apply, and therefore the ease and convenience of science makes us give our listening ears to the scientists who speak about the meaning of life, and move away from the complexities of religious or philosophical information which parts of it cannot be understood or perhaps conflicts with that which is proven in science. This conflict creates confusion in our minds, therefore our minds tend to give our listening ears to scientists who speak about the meaning of life, perhaps their answers might be simpler than the interlinks which are provided by experimental science.

Emotional Attachment to Science

It is noticeable that some people buy the products of famous brands which they do not need, including well-known brands of clothes, or electronic products. We find that in the days of discounts or on the dates of release of new product lines, people line up at those stores to buy brands or phones, driven by their emotions, and their previous experience which made them love the product. Lining up and waiting, not knowing whether their sizes are available or not, they feel that these brands can only produce perfect and flawless products. Those who observe them know that the association of their emotions with these products makes their purchasing decisions far from logical and rational.

These are the same sentiments that make those who have high regard for science hold on to waiting for a scientific answer to the meaning of his existence. This is because science is the manufacturer of the devices that take us to far places, the maker of the plane flying us over the clouds, and the binoculars that show us the wide edges of the universe. Science is the maker of technology and is part of the meanings of our lives, which we already talked about. It is natural for us to be attached to it as we are attached to money, children and the other meanings of life. Therefore, there are so many emotions that curve us from rational thinking when we are searching for the meaning of life, make us stick to science as brand fans stick to their favourite products. However, the fans of products, clothes and electronics have less emotional attachment to their products than those who hold science and scientists in high regard. The standing of the fans of these brands and their line up in front of their favourite stores is an acceptable matter, because the shop will eventually open the doors for them to enter and they may find what they are seeking, and it will not harm them to wait for a period of time. While those who hold high regard for science will be standing in front of the science shop for their entire life waiting for a product that has not yet been produced!

The Result

Scientists are not superhuman beings, however they can create super work teams, as the final result of their combined contributions over the years and centuries is close to being miraculous. When we go back to the historical sequences that enabled scientists to revolutionize any science, we find the chain to be clear whether it is physics, chemistry, biology or astronomy. We can see clearly how scientists complement each other, especially in the experimental sciences. But, when any of them work on the meaning of life, they work alone without the controls of the collective, and contributions from others, and therefore the results of their work is uncontrolled and poor/weak. Of all mankind's achievements in science to date, it has not enabled professional scientists to provide a concept for the meaning of life, and the data is not enough to form a conviction or theory.

No one can argue against the fact that science has made progress in the field of the emergence of life, evolution, the emergence of the universe, and also within many sciences, including chemistry and physics. However, the use of these results does not guide us to the meaning of our lives and we cannot rely on these achievements to build a theory that combines all the meanings that surround our lives. But the years and centuries to come are hiding much science from us, and many sciences will mature in the future, will be complete in all aspects, and after we learn about the relations of science with each other and their implications on our lives, we might then be able to be guided by science to build a theory that is based on evidence and facts and end up with results that explain the existence of all those meanings in our lives and present us with the basket that will contain all of it. The meaning of our existence may be hidden in one of those sciences, but we must be aware that waiting for those years or centuries to know is inadequate. What is the value of knowing the meaning of life when we are among the dead?

What the few scientists examined above say is nothing more than a sort of confusion of our understanding of the meaning of life. It is not wise to close our minds to the information provided by experimental science, as this would be closing our minds to sources that may guide us to the reasons of our existence. As for what we have learned today from science is partial, incomplete and not able to guide us by itself. If we insist on holding onto the idea that science is enough to guide us to the meaning of life, the result is that the meaning of life becomes for us a repository of genes (the view of some evolutionists) or that life has no meaning, we exist just like mountains. These are unscientific results and I refuse to credit it to science, as this reduces the value of science. Science is innocent of that statement, science will guide us someday to a better way of understanding the meaning of our lives.

We will not leave science because it has not guided us to the meaning of life, but we will continue to take from science what we can, and we will continue to look for solutions to our problems within research papers and the works of specialized scientists. But, we have to find an answer to the question of the meaning of life in another direction.

Note :

This section of the book is a reminder first to myself who loves science, and a reminder to all those who hold high regard for science, that science (currently) is not enough to answer the question of the meaning of life, and waiting for science to provide an answer is like a lifelong wait in front of a store that has not yet produced that product we so desire. We must search for it in other stores. We do not have to put ourselves in the position of choosing between science and ignorance, and when we search for the meaning of life in a non-science shop, we are not necessarily buying the meaning for our lives from an "ignorance shop". I may be a savvy, scientifically-knowledgeable person, and I make sure I have the latest inventions even if they cost high prices, and I am often a source of advice for my friends when they are looking for technological solutions for their homes or for their problems. However, I am aware of my emotional connection to science, and I try not to go beyond buying a phone or testing a new product, and what the reader experienced in the previous lines of criticism for science, is only an objective scientific discussion, stripping of myself, my belonging and love for science. Without this stripping, I would not have been able to critique and discuss science in objective discussions.

Chapter 3

Philosophy

Philosophers' theories about the meaning of life are divided in terms of the hypotheses that they propose during the formulation of their theories.[40] Some philosophers (super naturalists) propose that God is the centre of the universe; that God has a plan for people;[41] and that people should fulfil this plan. Also, some philosophers believe that He is the only way to evitate our existing as a result of chance, and therefore the meaning of our lives is based upon the existence of God.[42] Therefore, faith in God is an inevitable result of having a meaning in our lives.

As for philosophers who do not presume the existence of God (naturalists), these are philosophers who deal with what is constant in our materialistic, known and viewed world. They don't presume the existence of the spiritual world. Their theories are based on the assumption that nature manages the universe

---

[40] T. Metz, 'The Meaning of Life', The Stanford Encyclopedia of Philosophy (Summer 2013 Edition), Edward N. Zalta (ed.), https://plato.stanford.edu/archives/sum2013/entries/life-meaning/#Obj, (accessed 30 June 2017).

[41] J. Affolter, 'Human Nature as God's Purpose', Religious Studies, vol. 43, no. 4, 2007, pp. 443–455.

[42] W. Craig, 'The Absurdity of Life without God', in E. D. Klemke (ed.), The Meaning of Life, 2nd edn., Oxford University Press, New York, 2000, pp. 40–56.

without any need for the existence of a god. They argue whether meaning is really necessary for the makeup of our minds, and whether it should be a uniform meaning for all people.[43]

But, they are searching for a meaning for our existence. Some[44] of them believe that the variation of the meaning of life is a result of the variables and constants of one person or another. Whenever a person gets his desires granted, his life assumes more meaning for him.

Also, some claim that there are no constant standards for meaning; desires, purposes and the number of choices available to each person vary from one person to another.[45]

There is another section of philosophers (pessimists or nihilists) who believe that man will perish and turn to nothing. Their theories are about the idea that the meaning of man's life either does not exist, or that we cannot obtain the meaning of our

---

[43] Metz, loc. cit.

[44] B. A. Trisel, 'Futility and the Meaning of Life Debate', Sorites, no.14, 2002, pp. 70–84; B. Hooker, 'The Meaning of Life: Subjectivism, Objectivism, and Divine Support', in N. Athanassoulis and S. Vice (eds.) The Moral Life: Essays in Honour of John Cottingham, Palgrave Macmillan, New York, 2008, pp. 184–200. and A. Alexis, The Meaning of Life: A Modern Secular Answer to the Age-Old Fundamental Question, CreateSpace Independent Publishing Platform, USA, 2011.

[45] Metz, loc. cit.

life.[46] They do not presume the existence of the spiritual world, and many of them, as well, do not accept the existence of any importance of the human kind.

Martin Heidegger[47] says that the rest of the creatures might wonder about their situations, and regard the latter as a problem for which they are seeking a solution, whereas man regards his existence as a query and a source of anxiety, as a spring of hope, a gift, or an absurdity.

Schopenhauer[48] sees that only a fool could imagine that life deserves to be lived, and sees that the symbol that best expresses the human project is a camel; it digs into the ground actively and diligently with its big hooves, and that is the task of its entire life, wrapped with an eternal darkness. What does it gain from the process of this life, which is heaped with affliction and devoid of pleasure? Nutrition and reproduction are the only two ways of going on and starting over, through a new individual, with the same melancholic fate.

---

[46] Trisel, *loc. cit.*

Hooker, *loc. cit.*

Alexis, *loc. cit.*

[47] M. Heidegger, Being and Time, State University of New York Press, New York, 1996, cited in T. Eagleton, The Meaning of Life, Oxford University Press, New York, 2007.

[48] T. Eagleton, The Meaning of Life. Translated to Arabic by Ahd Ali Al-Deeb, Dar Al-Farqad, 2010.

He says that it is obvious how the entire human project is a terrible mistake which should have been corrected a long time ago. Only he whose mind has dulled, and has been fooled by his ego, can imagine otherwise on facing the tomb of history. He adds that the story of man is that of a misery pressing on the chest, and only those who have been fooled by the despicable cunning of the will consider it worthy of seeing the light.

Terry Eagleton says in his book *The Meaning of Life*[49] that whoever assumes that life comprises a higher meaning has to face the serious challenge posed by Schopenhauer[50]; that he needs to exert a tremendous effort to make life anything but palliative consolation.

He also says[51] that if we were obliged to search into the meaning of existence (the collective existence of all people) on a broad scale, our search will probably fail. But, if we search into the personal meaning of existence of one person, that is another matter. As he says in his book *The Meaning of Life*[52], "man's existence is casual, meaning that it lacks foundation, aim, purpose or necessity, and that human kind could have so easily not appeared on the face of the Earth at all. This probability

---

[49] Ibid.
[50] German philosopher (1788 – 1860).
[51] Eagleton, loc. cit.
[52] Ibid.

empties our actual existence from its essence, and casts upon it a permanent shadow of loss and death. Even in our most ecstatic moments, we are tragically aware that the ground is wobbling underneath our feet, and that there is no solid foundation for what we are and what we do. This is what could add more value to our good times, or could contribute to demeaning their value significantly."

This is some of what pessimistic philosophers brought. There is no doubt that both ancient and modern philosophers have a lot to say about the meaning of life. It's their court and their field. Whoever has presented a meaning of life, has taken support from the ideas of religion, and from the fact that the existence of meaning arises from the presence of a divine will that makes life logical and meaningful. Whoever didn't take support from religion was closer to a wonderer than a responder to the question about the meaning of life.

Chapter 4

Openness

If we try to identify the concept of Faith in the minds of human beings we find a great difference, for all of us have been subjected to a previous experience which painted in our minds, a mental image of religion, and this mental image works like a lens through which we see religious topics. Our previous experiences are what determines the shape of the lens we have of divine messages, and this book presents the concept of divine messages differently from most of our previous understandings. The divine messages that are referred to in this book are Islam, Judaism and Christianity; the messages that came from God and still exist today. The concept is shared by all the divine messages, and the concept of the messages about the meaning of life may differ from the concept of each message separately. As we all have different experiences with regards to the divine, we need to clarify a set of matters before we start talking about the meaning of life with regards to divine messages. The divine messages, although they differ greatly in their applications and practices, are very similar in their concept of life and its meaning. We must redraw the concept of the divine messages from a whole new angle to many of us, and because this book is another experience that will be added to the reader's experience, therefore, we need to draw a new form and features for the concept of the divine messages. There is no doubt that we have all received some information during our lives that painted a different image of religion for each of us. It is natural for any reader to feel confused, and we can't help but be affected by what was previously painted in our imagination. If the reader is a Jew, his Jewish instructions will not be omitted, and if he is a Muslim or a Christian or a Buddhist or Confucian, he will be affected as well, and even the atheist will evoke his concept of religion, or will evoke his objections to religion to see the divine messages. Because I write to make a difference to those who read my book, I will not enter into discussion about religion without making sure that the reader is ready to rule out everything that was previously painted in his mind, and give me the opportunity to draw what I want, and then the reader has the option to dismiss my views and return to his own views. Are you ready to do this?

Are you ready to open your mind to a new picture?

Be a Guest in My House

I live in a country where most of its inhabitants do not enjoy drinking soda water. When I welcome my guests, I honour them in the way I see fit. My house guests will usually get a fresh cup of coffee that I roasted and ground myself, and with it a piece of Belgian chocolate and a bottle of soda water, which is something that I myself enjoy. After they open the bottle and taste the water, their faces show signs of displeasure, and I have discovered the reason. So, after they open the bottle of the soda water I tell them this is not a sweet soda drink as they may be used to. This is simply water with gas, there is no trace of sugar. Once they know this, the signs of displeasure disappear from their faces, and they become more receptive to it. Their minds immediately refer to their previous experiences, and because they see the gases in it, their minds tells them the nearest thing it knows, this is 7-up or Sprite. So of course, when they taste the drink and it isn't sweet, these perceptions, these prior judgments make them feel displeasure when drinking water that is free of sugar. And here, you are the guest of my book, will you allow me to offer some guidance in the way I address the meaning of the "gas" of life which I present, which is the food of the mind?

Allow difference to happen

I write to make a difference to the meaning of life in my reader's mind. Making a difference is not easy, the mind of the reader who is reading my book now is a mind that has already formed its formula of the meaning of life as Terry Eagleton said in his book *The Meaning of Life*, "We will find that each individual has formed a formula of his own". It cannot be overlooked that the meaning of life for the respectful reader has led to the organization of his life, as Eagleton also said [53] "All their opinions, methods, behaviour, movements, expressions,

---

[53] T. Eagleton, The Meaning of Life. Translated to Arabic by Ahmad Ali Deeb, Dar Al-Farqad, 2010.

etiquette, ambitions and customs are in line with the formula which they have formulated for themselves about the meaning of life."

Distinguished readers will review their convictions, and present them for analysis, but they need a lot of detachment to reach the taste of the soda water that I am about to pour in their cups (minds). Their minds are occupied by their previous convictions, and will receive the new information as my guests would receive the soda water, expecting it be a sweet soda drink, as our minds will also make a lot of misconceptions. Therefore, I will give you some remedies that have succeeded in washing the mental vessel, so that your vessel may be clean and open to new concepts, and that is when I reveal some of the errors that occur in our minds when we talk about the meaning of life, our mind is not a blank white paper, we are mature people, and we have our convictions, ideas and experiences that have somehow turned into pillars which our lives stand on. However, another part of our minds does not want to demolish what has been built in the past, and there are other reasons which I will be addressing in detail later.

How opened minded are you?

During the graduate studies of Business

Administration, a Professor of one of the courses told us that he writes for 16 hours a day. At the time I did not have any affection for writing. I simply did not like it, so I asked him: What attracts you to writing? He said "creation", then he explained to me how writing makes him feel the beauty of creating a scientific matter from nothing, his words were the key words that made me leave the seat of a reader and move to the seat of a writer, and I have found much beauty there. It is true that my motives now are different than his motives, what motivates me to write is "to make a positive impact on the reader" not "creation", however, moving out of my observing position and trying to observe what others do, made me see that there was a better observing position than my previous one. I do not have to sit where others are sitting and observing, instead I have found a different and better place, and so the same can be true in life. To be open to others' opinion is the secret of those who are successful in life. From my personal observation, those who are the most open to others' opinion are the most successful, but full openness to others' opinion is theoretical rather than being a fact. Imagine with me that you were crossing a road and when the traffic light allowed you to cross, you were hit by a vehicle. The driver passed the red light, the loss of his job and receiving the news of his son's death caused him to miss the traffic light and due to these concerns made him lose concentration and end up driving right into your path while you were crossing. He may tell you his reasons, but regardless of just how open you are at the moment, you will not be able to pardon him. You may pardon him at a later date, but not at the moment of the accident, as we do not want to see the facts at that time. This is because we are under the pressure of our daily endurance, our endless needs and our unfulfilled goals.

Openness is about a change in the observing position from which we observe the events of our lives. But, changing the observing position in many situations of life is as difficult as forgiving a driver who has run a red light, knocked you down and broken your leg. While you're lying there in pain, changing your observing position is incredibly hard. Only later, looking back does this become easier. So we see, in life, the circumstances surrounding us may be obstacles to openness.

Openness to ideas and beliefs will remain limited to our past practice of openness which has defined our capacity for openness. Openness is like a sport, we need to practice it every day to get the best ability to be open to others' ideas after some time, and the challenge of 'a complete openness' is a big challenge. It depends on our real desire to leave what we are currently observing, and move away from the position of our observations and then observe the same scene from a different angle.

Whatever our scientific or academic level, doubting and questioning our own ideas, and those of others, is what helps us to move our position of observance and open our minds. For some people who have spent their lives with a very closed view, this can be hard, but allowing yourself to understand the viewpoint of others, and see everything from a different angle is so beneficial to understanding yourself and the world around you.

The Sharp Knife

Research shows that people consistently doubt evidence that they learn about second-hand but do not themselves see; witnessed events are much easier to believe than ones only heard of. Further, people tend to be more doubtful of results when they are against their current beliefs, though less so when the results affirm their current beliefs and to cast less doubt when the results are positive. However, we witness this sort of behaviour and judgments every day.

When we visit a doctor and he advises us to rest for three days and to apply an ointment, most of us will not be sceptical about that. On the other hand, most of us will consult another physician when he informs us – God forbid – that we have an incurable disease. We would all cast doubt upon the diagnosis and prescription of that physician, because the diagnosis he provided may have been inaccurate.

Doubt is the path that has led us to all the sciences we have established, through what is called critical thinking. Critical thinking has taught us how to achieve advances in those sciences; how to distinguish between facts and between hypotheses that are unsupported by evidence; and to dismiss the latter. Doubt is the cure to our ignorance, but it is also the disease. This book doesn't educate us about the conclusions of scientific research. The solid proof, of which the experimental method can be replicated, is not to be found amidst the pages of this book. And if it were, then science would be capable of bringing us to it, and I would spend my holiday playing cards with my children and would neglect writing. If science has proved the issue by experiment, why then should I write?

A person with a critical mindset, and who masters critical thinking, has a sharp, knife-like mind, which can tear through any topic. It's true that I invite the reader to learn, but I am also eager for him or her to benefit and profit. So many times, have I held the knife of my criticism, hurt my hand, and deprived myself of the benefit.

In my book *The 5 Essential Dimensions* , I related the story of my treatment from a slipped neck disc, which had been prescribed to me by my doctor. Nevertheless, my doubts about the prescribed therapy kept me from complying with it. After having consulted an expert, I took up the therapy - which resulted in relief from my painful condition.

In so many situations I was hesitant to take a step forward; my doubtfulness stood in the way. I couldn't let go of my sharp knife. I have never seen a person of sound judgment who has been delivered from his knife. Someone might be irritable, because their meticulousness is pressuring them or turning them off from the matter in hand. Another one may be thinking too much about a trivial matter, because of his meticulousness. A third one is doubtful of a story told by an honest person 'who had witnessed the events himself'. The former won't believe the latter, for the former doesn't want to question his own convictions. So he takes the effortless way of doubting the stories of others, even if they were honest - although no disaster would hit him if he believed those stories.

There are numerous analogies of rational people, the sharp knives of whose brains cut their benefits away from them. This book presents logical and solid conclusions, but they remain mere conclusions. Some people will be more likely to question these conclusions if they oppose some of their beliefs. So, are you one of those people?

When we are discussing with someone a certain topic, about which we have different opinions and predetermined convictions, it is then supposed that there will be some kind of hindrance. Our minds do not seek facts, but strive to affirm the information we already have. We should be aware of the fact that to become convinced of something, about which we already have a different point of view, requires a double mental effort. The hindrance is considerable. Meanwhile, to become convinced of something that opposes our daily life practices, requires a sincere desire to know the truth no matter the cost.

Predetermined Convictions

Many people do not know that the German Nazis (1920 – 1945) used to advocate animal protection and welfare, and supported animal rights. The Nazis[54] were one of the first governments to set animal rights laws. Promoting any positive aspects of Nazism could not be seen as an upside, even if these positive aspects were true. The hideous practices of the Nazis will restrict our ability to open up. Our minds will be tied up with the ropes of their hideousness that would hinder our opening up and seeing facts.

I have given you this instance in order to illustrate how hindrances affect our brains and block us from seeing facts. Our minds will try to cloud our vision of any good thing the Nazis may have done. Due to our predetermined convictions concerning the concentration camps and the holocaust – regardless of any good thing the Nazis may have done, our minds will not want to see the truth about the whole picture, and will not want to check its validity.

Unseen Hindrances

Talking about religion and beliefs will never escape from our predetermined convictions. We often recall our 'prior problems' with the heavenly books.

---

54 Wikipedia contributors, "Animal welfare in Nazi Germany", Wikipedia The Free Encyclopedia, [website], last edited 14 September 2017, https://en.wikipedia.org/wiki/Animal_welfare_in_Nazi_Germany, (accessed 16 September 2017).

Somewhat subconsciously, our minds hinder our opening up to other ideas and beliefs. Our minds will try to hinder the process of 'shifting the centre of focus'. Therefore, we ought to be aware of the hindrance set by our minds against our opening up.

A Hair from a Pig's Back

Arabic proverbs have profound significance that cut long conversations and detailed descriptions short. In the Arabian Peninsula, we do not eat ham products.

We believe pigs are unclean and so we avoid them. However, a rational person will not deprive himself of some benefit even if it lies in a place he doesn't like or with a person whom he does not want to deal with. If an elderly person wanted to encourage a young man to move forward and benefit from a horrible person, that elder would tell the young man, "A hair from a pig's back is beneficial."

Likewise, the greater benefits in life might be lying in the places that we detest the most. Our most enchanting situation could take place in a graveyard – and the greatest benefit might come from an annoying person, as the British say "don't cut your nose off to spite your face".

Examples of Hindrances to Openness

Hindrances will vary according to the centre of focus of every reader reading this book. A Muslim reader will recall his objections to the scriptures of the Old Testament and its verses about the meaning of life. He will allege that wisdom is confined to the Holy Quran, and forget Allah's words in the latter about the Old Testament, "And how will they make thee *their* judge when they have with them the Torah,...wherein was guidance and light".[55]

Similarly, a Jewish or a Christian may recall their disagreements as well when I cite verses from the Quran. One of the problems might be women wearing the *niqab*,[56] or whatever problem it might be.

I invite all those whose objections will hinder them from stepping out of their safe zone, and behold the Quran verses from the optimum centre of focus, gain insight into the meanings of those verses, and benefit from them. After having the full experience, the reader could revert to his/her previous point and search into their dilemmas. Maybe it wasn't Allah that commanded wearing the *niqab* in any verse; it was the understanding of the preachers that advocated the *niqab*. Let's keep in mind that this book is not itself looking into any

---

[55] (Al-Ma'eidah: 44, 45).

[56] "A niqab is a garment of clothing that covers the face which is worn by a small minority of Muslim women as a part of a particular interpretation of hijab ("modesty")."

Wikipedia contributors, "Niqab", Wikipedia The Free Encyclopedia, [website], last version 14 September 2017,

https://en.wikipedia.org/w/index.php?title=Niq%C4%81b&oldid=802163545, (accessed 24/9/2017).

dilemmas, but it aims to present the meaning in life that all divine messages have agreed upon. All those who will go through the full experience will benefit, and those who won't will lose.

The hindrance of a non-believer or an atheist is different. His prior problems with religions will come to his mind when I review some verses from the Old Testament or from the Quran. He will wonder where God is amidst all the injustice and murder that has happened and is happening.

I encourage him to put aside this question temporarily, and step out of his safe zone to be able to see the benefits of meaning to his emotional and mental wellbeing. Then, let him decide for himself if religions present a meaning in life or not. Afterwards, he could revert to his atheism or beliefs whenever he wants – after he has seen these things from a different centre of focus, and has lived the experience "fully" and entirely, so as to be able to view his life and its meanings from that different centre of focus.

Rules of Customary Passions

It seems that the Scottish philosopher David Hume's words that reason is the slave of passion, "Reason is, and ought only to be the slave of the passions"[57] is right. Human beings justify every moral or immoral act they do; passions and motives are the ones who decide, and reason is the one which fulfils our desires. Imagine that you are a judge eager to judge with integrity, and when you reach the age of seventy, one of the lawyers who is the same age as your own children comes to guide you on a legal rule which you were not aware of and if you had known about it, dozens of prisoners would not have gone to prison. Would you accept that you were wrong, to the extent that you have sent dozens of people to prison when they were not supposed to be sent to prison? It is possible that you will be able to admit your mistake, but do not be surprised that the majority will look for a legal justification which makes the image in his mind, which is 'The Hero Judge' to be the sound image, and will not accept that his image is the image of a 'stupid' person sitting on the seat of a judge. Regardless how receptive we are to other's opinion, the openness to other's opinion that would result in the 'obliteration of our image', our minds will shut the way to such openness involuntarily, and will reject it, because if we accept it, we accept the obliteration of our image to ourselves. We will look for a justification for what we are doing, and we will fight to keep the people we have thrown in prison as prisoners who are not innocent. We will look for reasons that make our image in

---

[57] D. Hume, *A treatise of human nature*, in D. D. Raphael, *British Moralists 1650 – 1800*, Hackett Publishing, Indianapolis, Indiana, 1969.

our eyes not that bad, and we shall not forget that there are those who have the courage to go to prison and apologize to those who they wronged and announce their mistakes to all. Are you one of them?

When we read any topic that leads us to become unjust or ignorant or trivial, our reading will be logical whereas logic is under the customary rule of passion, and under our motives for not losing our previous self-image. When our mind doubts that the subject 'may' bring to our image any loss, it will not push us towards the verification of the received information, and if we do verify it, we will question its legitimacy, and if it could not find anything that justifies what it does, it will deter us from progressing towards full and complete openness and join forces with the passion of 'hatred to lose' of our involuntary minds. This will then help to impede being open to seeing our losses, and when our losses consist of entire years of life and past convictions, our minds and emotions will hate that to happen, and therefore our emotions will try their best for us to not step out of our position, and what we will see is, at best, 'our great loss', so why step out? Self-preservation often wins out over openness.

The search for the meaning of life might lead us to be insignificant for decades, are we ready to be insignificant? We all want the truth, however there is no doubt that when the price of accepting the truth is our vanity or to be seen as a naïve person for many years. Some will complete the book, but search for another book that makes their own conviction better, their entire years of life more beneficial and their minds more aware. They may look for critics who challenge the book and support them. Justifying to themselves that they are not alone, dozens do not agree with those ideas, but I am sure there are many other people who could sacrifice everything they have to know the truth; therefore, I shall keep writing for them.

My Loving Friend

I have a friend in my neighbourhood, a man about the age of seventy, who is great to converse with. We discuss many ideas, he has a good way with words. I often used to meet him and after a meeting and discussions with him, I gave him a copy of my book 5 *Essential Dimensions*. I met him two months later, and he had only read 10 pages of the book and had written scathing comments on the margins of the book. The comments were illogical, and I was surprised with his behaviour, and when we discussed it, he told me that I was talking about topics which I do not have knowledge about. When I asked him about it, in an attempt to clarify the points that he raised about my book, I realized that he was not listening to me as he always had done before. I returned to the copy of the book and to his comments and found them extremely naive. I checked myself, I might have changed and became a person who does not like to hear criticism whereas I was passionate and eager to hear it before, but his criticism did not exceed a set of observations that do not amount to criticism, as criticism is a position of weakness that will become in the future a position of construction, and that is what brings me benefits, while praises and compliments are no more than passing pleasure. I do not usually get surprised at any criticism, no matter how bad it may be. There are a lot of psychological reasons that make others criticize me, such as jealousy or to prove their knowledge or further themselves from ignorance, and yet the bad and scathing criticism often is useful to me. Where I spend my time thinking of the criticism that is mixed with insults and hurt, and after I push aside my emotions, I can extract benefits from the scathing criticism, but his criticism was without any benefit. I was very surprised that this person did this. It is a gesture that I did not see in him in the past, and despite my repeated review of all his comments, I did not find the benefits. How could he criticize me when I know that he loves me? I was confused and amazed about his motives as he loves me no doubt. How could he do that? He is the same person who praised me and complimented me to my face and in my absence and to this day, two years after my first book.

After many reflections of the possibilities and comparing them with the comments that he wrote on my book, I realized that he did not understand my book, as my writings are for the highly intellectual elite. It was not suitable for him, so when he tried to read my book and did not understand, he put himself in a difficult position. He had to choose between two options, either I do not write well, or his life of seventy years does not enable him to understand the book written by someone who is the same age as his sons. Therefore he chose the first option, and decided to keep the beautiful picture of himself in his mind, maintaining the image of the educated intellectual.

My previous story embodies the challenge of full openness. Some will hesitate to complete the search for the truth in any matter if it leads to his loss.

Imagine someone who buys a house. The down payment for this house is half their life savings. This down payment is non-refundable. Now let's say that after having paid this down payment, he reads the news that the neighbourhood has a high crime rate. He may decide to forget about his down payment and leave the neighbourhood, however many will choose not to investigate the news when they've have reached this level of commitment, and if they do discover this information, they will doubt it. You see there is a huge motive not to see the truth. That motive is half of their wealth. Such a loss may be tangible and real, as the house deposit or down payment, or it may be a moral and perceived as the image of the intellectual man and the fair judge, therefore, the meaning of life may make our previous life seem a great loss. Should we uphold the truth that shows us the meaning of life to come, or hold on to our previous illusions?

Our Previous Knowledge Prevents Us From Learning

I have a friend, he is married to a Doctor, and between them they have a lot of dietary and weight-loss knowledge. I went out with him one day for a walk, and he complained to me about his repeated attempts to lose weight. I tried to tell him about my successful experience with weight loss, and explained simple steps to help him to lose weight. He interrupted me with his inputs more than once, as his knowledge of diet and nutrition is vast and every time I tried to explain the mistake he might be making, his interruptions to me became more frequent and I could not give him any information. I overcame my own feelings of discomfort with the situation and then I said to him: If what you know benefits you, why don't you tell me why you could not lose weight in five years? He became silent and I stopped talking to him, and then he gave me some attention, to listen to what I had to say. I said to him, the thing that you do not know is that the knowledge you have may be an obstacle to progress in the process of reducing your weight. Then he gave me his full attention. I requested from him two things. First to erase from his mind all the information he knows about weight-loss and secondly to listen to my advice. I met him after a week and his weight had decreased. This story with my friend is a story I see repeated every day. Many of us know that they do not have a clear and definite meaning, but they stick to the meaning that they have, and if they read my book, they will not leave their previous information about the meaning of life, and their previous information about the meaning of life might prevent them from benefiting from my book.

Do You Have Intellectual Viruses?

Some young people believe that life is a combination of pleasures or multiple adventures and when someone comes to them to talk to them about buying a house, where they should make a commitment for many years for the purpose of saving, a direct rejection will be the response from most of them. Their desire to enjoy life and buy what they desire for themselves will contradict the idea of saving for the future; it runs against the outlines of their convictions about life. Often opportunity comes, but we miss it because we don't have enough openness. For example, those mental viruses prevent us from seeing the great opportunity of buying our dream house where the house prices have risen 40% for last few decades; just because it is outside the border of philosophy, framework, where those viruses become hyperactive and prevent us from seeing the full picture of any opportunity.

The openness to ideas that oppose our broad lines of life are evident in many young people's practices, but they are more flexible in changing their "philosophical" attitudes when they begin to understand that saving is important. But, they delay it. Older people practice it more widely, and the preventing viruses that they have are stronger and more powerful, the foundation on which they built on, they do not want to destroy what is above it.

The search for intellectual viruses in our minds is like searching for harmful bacteria in our bodies. We do not need to make sure that they exist or to doubt it, they exist without a doubt in my mind and in all our minds. Let's look at their effect on us, it exists and is active under our lives' philosophical brink which we build on. Let's take control measures for our thoughts that start to oppose, once the new thoughts intersect with the broad lines of our lives. When these viruses are activated to refute the new thoughts, and prevent us from complete openness to them and use doubt to keep us from being open to them, to identify how they work to obstruct the openness and prevent us from completing our journey to search for the truth. Let's leave the gravity of the orbit of our old thoughts.

To challenge our philosophy, it makes us see ourselves and our philosophies from other angles. Like someone who is travelling in the space of knowledge to see the reality of his planet and to see his life from multiple angles, and this does not happen unless we leave the gravity of our philosophy. However, few of us do challenge and try to change it, even if they tried, they would find that their lives had lost meaning and they do not want to know another. Very few of us write their convictions and philosophies of life on paper, so when they reject some of what is written in this book, they might not see that their rejection is as a result of its opposition with their convictions. So, as with all subjects, let's give them the right to be considered and be reflected on before we judge them. Our full openness for new ideas will not prevent us from returning to our previous beliefs and convictions, we will return to them after a real experience of new ideas, and making sure to consider whether the new idea is true or incorrect.

The Rebellion Against our Emotions

We can overcome this rebellion of emotions if we show it the full picture of our loss equation. There is a big potential profit as well, as we can overcome its obstruction by reminding ourselves that our departure from our convictions is a temporary departure and will not exceed the period of the experience. Our memories from our book will be as the memories of a trip to the Alps for a week leaving all our comfort zones, and trying something completely new to us. We will return to our previous convictions as we return to the comfort of our own homes after the journey and the adventure. Openness to new ideas will not prevent us from a return to our old ideas, we will enjoy a fascinating view of life, as someone who is enjoying the magnificent scenery of the Alps. We will not enjoy the most beautiful memories simply through watching TV programs about the Alps. A complete experience is the only way to create memories that move emotions. Let us leave our old orbit gravity, let's travel on an enjoyable journey, and create all the memories from the upcoming pages.

Chapter 5

Faith (The Divine Messages)

Does Faith Offer a Meaning of Life?

Faith offers a meaning of life. The researcher Pargamant (1997) says that religion is the search for the meaning of life in a sacred way,[58] and that agrees with the conclusion of Dariusz Krok[59] that religion offers a set of meanings and the utmost motives for all events of life. It gives us goals and provides a value system that helps to explore the meanings of life gradually and religious beliefs, emotions and practices are an integral part of the series of meanings of life. They contribute to overcoming the difficulties and challenges of life,[60] and that is in accord with what the researchers Bargeman (2005)[61] and Park (2005)[62] have proven.

---

[58] K. I. Pargament, *The Psychology of Religion and Coping*, Guilford Press, New York, 1997.

[59] D. Krok, 'The Role of Meaning in Life Within the Relations of Religious Coping and Psychological Well-Being', *Journal of Religion and Health,* vol. 54, no. 6, 2015, pp. 2292–2308.

[60] *Ibid.*

[61] Pargament, *loc. cit.*

[62] C. L. Park, 'Religion as a Meaning-making Framework in Coping with Life Stress', *Journal of Social Issues,* vol. 61, no. 4, 2005, pp. 707–729.

The Four Premises of Faith

When we combine the various religion's divine messages together, searching for the one theory contained in them all, then the resulting theory will present the results. While the results may vary from what we have learned, generally the centre of this theory is present in all of the divine messages. The consensus of the divine messages is that faith is the belief and trust that the universe has a creator, and this faith may be based on four premises. The first is the existence of a creator who started the creation. The second premise is that the creator wanted there not to be any empirical evidence of his existence. The third premise is that he is excellent in what he does, and the fourth premise is that he created us for the purpose of testing us. These four presumptions which all faith is based on provide the reasons for our short existence in the context of the test, and introduce the 'recognition' of the creator, the realization of which is to be the objective of our existence.

Life as a Product

Faith offers the meaning of life as a temporary and transitory life, and it presents our existence as a gift and blessing from God. The divine messages agree on the subject of believing in the unknown, and that is to believe that God exists without seeing him. The messages also agree that our lives are temporary and transitory, and that after death will be the eternal and ever-lasting life. The metaphor of the meaning of life in the context of faith is that faith offers also the 'experience of life' as an experiment to test our reactions. As God says in the *Qur'an* "[He] who created death and life to test you [as to] which of you is best indeed"[63] and in *The Old Testament* "when he hath tried me, I shall come forth as gold",[64] this life that we see and watch is not a complete life, as it is an experience similar to experiencing a product before it is bought, as we are under testing, and who believes in the unknown, deserves the eternal life in heaven. So therefore, the believers live in an exceptional life 'under the context of the test' and therefore they state they are living now and the life they see is not an authentic life, but an exceptional situation. The authentic life is a full life without its defects and limitations such as extinction, misery and loss. These are deliberate and intentional defects in order to motivate humans to buy the complete version of their own life 'the eternal life' and the price of this eternal life is to believe in its existence and to seek it.

Risk of losing what is important to us in this life is always considered by nearly everyone. We are scared of losing our wealth, so we prepare for the risks, diversify investments, and increase savings. Our loved ones also mean a lot to us, we fear for them from the accidents of life and its calamities and we fear

---

[63] SAHIH INTERNATIONAL, http://www.alquranenglish.com/quransurah-al-mulk-2-qs-67-2-in-arabic-and-english-translation.

[64] (Job 23:10 NKJV)

our life partner may not love us any more, that he or she might change on us. We wish to remain and continue all existing meanings; whilst we are convinced they will vanish. Faith makes us see the giver of those meanings and the giver is able to preserve for us what is important to us and keep them eternally with us. "They are in what they desire themselves eternally".[65] and in *The Old Testament*'s Book of Daniel: "... some to eternal life".[66]

Is it Logical for the Empirical Evidence to be Absent?

The absence of empirical evidence is a very logical matter; as the testable evidence contradicts one of the four presumptions underlying the 'theory of faith' and when we have empirical evidence that proves God's existence, believing of the unknown becomes meaningless.

The presumption of the test makes life a test room, imagine you are sitting in a room and have an exam paper with a set of questions, but the question with the highest points value is "Do you believe in your Creator without seeing Him?" Could you ask the test supervisors to provide evidence of God's existence? This

---

[65] SAHIH INTERNATIONAL, http://www.alquranenglish.com/quransurah-al-anbiya-102-qs-21-102-in-arabic-and-english-translation.
[66] (Daniel 12:2 NKJV)

explains the absence of the evidence 'that can be tested' for it is God's desire and will, but the absence of empirical evidence does not mean the absence of evidence, as humans for hundreds of centuries recognize their Lord through opening the pages of his words and then opening their hearts and speaking to him, their eyes may tear when their lips are moving and saying, 'Guide us to you.'

Whoever wears the lens of faith will see that the creator of the universe wanted to be recognized away from any 'empirical' evidence that determines once and for all his existence. I have not found a clear and explicit text which reveals to us that God caused the lack of the existence of empirical evidence, and perhaps the reason is that whoever recognizes God, God loves them. Or perhaps when we recognize him, we will realize his powers and his greatness and therefore we fear him, and based on that, when God reveals to us his higher being and we recognize his existence, we will love him or fear him, and the test of recognizing him will end. Then comes the ability to follow his commands and move away from his prohibitions without seeing him, or perhaps God has many creations whom worshiped him, as God says in the *Quran* "The seven heavens and the earth and whatever is in them exalt Him. And there is not a thing except that it exalts [Allah] by His praise, but you do not understand their [way of] exalting. Indeed, He is ever

Forbearing and Forgiving"[67] and in the *Old Testament* "His angels ... the doers of his commands",[68] and they never stop worshiping him lovingly and fearfully and wanted to create a new creation to test them in recognizing him, these 'abstract' reasons, are not conclusive. However, what is conclusive is that creation of life has been created for ultimately a serious reason, and is not a game; and God is infallible from tampering as he says in the *Quran* "Then did you think that We created you uselessly and that to Us you would not be returned?"[69] and also says in the *Quran* "We did not create the heavens and earth and what is between them except in truth and [for] a specified term. But those who disbelieve, from that of which they are warned, are turning away."[70] We also see reason behind creation in *The Old Testament*, "The LORD by wisdom founded the earth, by understanding He established the heavens"[71] and they are not presented here to believe in them, it is to approximate the idea that our ignorance of reasons for creation, doesn't mean the lack of evidence altogether. Therefore, the believers know that logic

---

[67] Online Bible,

http://www.copticchurch.net/cgibin/bible/index.php?r=Daniel+1&version=NKJV&btn=View&showVN=1.

[68] Online Bible,

http://www.copticchurch.net/cgibin/bible/index.php?r=psalm+20&version=NKJV&btn=View&showVN=1.

[69] (Al Muminun: 115).

[70] (Al-Ahqaf:3).

[71] (Proverbs 3:19 ESV)

is for the created if it does exist, and the Creator must have reasons for the creation that they do not know, and when they know it, everything that happens to them will be logical. The absence of empirical evidence is one of those things that they do not know the reason for, but they believe in it, and the absence of empirical evidence for the creator does not mean the absence of evidence altogether, and the empirical evidence does exist in the historical events, testimonies of witnesses and miracles that happen. We find them in history and religious books and they are discussed in most universities. Whoever is able to use the lens of faith will understand the purpose of his existence among the living and will recognize his importance as concluded both Park and Bargeman (2005).[72]

The Purpose of Our Existence

Achieving the personal goals of our lives in this life and in the afterlife, are the objectives of our existence. God says, "But seek, through that which Allah has given you, the home of the Hereafter; and do not forget your share of this life",[73] and as it mentioned in *The Old Testament*: "Behold, that which I have seen good, which is good: for man to eat and drink and see good

---

[72] Park, *op.cit.*

[73] SAHIH INTERNATIONAL, http://www.alquranenglish.com/quransurah-al-qasas-77-qs-28-77-in-arabic-and-english-translation

from all his labours ... the days of his life"[74], therefore, religion provides in one way or another, understanding of the purpose of our existence and our importance, as concluded by both researchers Hood (2009) and Park (2013).[75]

The Meaning of Faith is Clear and Specific

Faith makes our existence in life a test and its reward is an eternal life. Or, as we said, it is a sample of the product and the reward is the product itself, this meaning gives us the basket that gathers life and its meanings. If we enjoy the pleasure of this life and see its meanings, we will recognize who gave it to us, and when we recognize the giver and try to achieve better results in his tests, because he is the only one who makes us last in it eternally with everything we love, and when we see the extension of those meanings, our focus will be shifted from sampling the product. We will be attached to our Creator, and we will not simply be attached to what he offers us, and only then we will see a meaning for our lives.

I received from social media a video of adults who saw colours for the first time in their lives. Some do not know what to say, some wonder and then rejoice and start jumping for joy. They

---

[74] (Ecclesiastes 5:18)

[75] C. L. Park, *Religion and meaning*, in R. F. Paloutzian & C. L. Park (Eds.), *Handbook of the Psychology of Religion and Spirituality*, The Guilford Press, New York, 2013, pp. 357–378.

feel grateful to those who gave them the gift, and who made the glasses that enabled them to see colours. I also watched another film about people who heard sounds for the first time, watching their excitement and emotions is an enjoyable thing, the lens of religion will show us that seeing, hearing, seeing colours and our existence among the living, as a gift from the Creator. Believers feel the feelings of those people every day, and in every bite of food they eat, in every breath they inhale in their lungs and every breath they exhale, and this feeling of gratitude makes them happier and reassured. When researchers asked participants in a study to write letters of gratitude[76] to people who had been good to them, the results were that those who wrote the letters experienced an improvement in their psychological state and were more satisfied and less depressed and happier, and so is the believer who practices religion in their lives because they write hundreds of "heart-felt" messages on a daily basis to their Creator, pleading, thanking and praising Him.

So, there are the meanings, believers see them in every bite of food, they feel grateful to He who created it for them and created them. They struggle and work to get food in this life, but He will feed them without working for it in the afterlife, He will give them water without thirst, and they believe that He who created

---

[76] S. M. Toepfer, K. Cichy & P. Peters, 'Letters of Gratitude: Further Evidence for Author Benefits', *Journal of Happiness Studies*, vol. 13, no. 1, 2012, pp 187-201, available at https://doi.org/10.1007/s10902-011-9257-7

them the first time is able to create them again complete, beautiful without beautification. There he will give them whatever they ask for, and as it is him who willed their pleasures in food to be less, he can will their pleasures to be great in heaven, and everything that bring them joy and happiness. It is that way because the creator willed it to be that way, and even though their life that is the basket that collects all meanings is short and with flaws and blended with ignorance, they spend their life learning. It is contaminated with sickness and they seek treatment, it is associated with young age and they wait to grow and mature with that growth, they are afraid of aging, and all these flaws can only be repaired by their creator and He is able to make it pure, complete and without diminution.

The Positives (Pros) of Faith

Happiness and contentment are of the most positive aspects of the meaning of life seen through the lens of religion. It is for many reasons, amongst them is what Chamberlain and Zika (1992)[77] have found, that religion helps people in their search for the meaning of life, [78] and as Hood (2009) also states that religion offers individuals a set of goals, meanings and beliefs

---

[77] S. Zika, & K. Chamberlain, 'On the Relation Between Meaning in Life and Psychological Well-being', *British Journal of Psychology*, vol. 83, 1992, pp. 133-145.
[78] R. W, Hood, et al., *The psychology of religion: An empirical approach*, 4th ed, Guilford, New York, 2009.

that provide an explanation and clarification for the complexities of life[79].

The Meaning of Life Emanates from the Knowledge of the Giver of Life

Faith distinguishes between authentic and impermanent aims. It categorizes the pleasure and happiness that we savour in various entities, such as food and drink, or our spouses and children, as perishable pleasures, and not as a true aim. A true aim is one that couldn't be ceased by death, be deranged by disease, or fade away with time.

A true aim is immortality in what the soul desires; as God says in the *Quran*, "and they will forever abide in what their hearts desire"[80] and in *The Old Testament* of *The Bible*, "...everyone whose name shall be found written in the book...shall awake...to everlasting life".[81] It is also the ultimate achievement; *"Whoever obeys* God and His Messenger has won a great victory".[82]

Faith stresses upon the fact that purposelessness does not count as one of the aims of our creation; we are created to be honoured and examined.

---

[79] *Ibid.*
[80] (Al-Anbiya 102).
[81] (Daniel 12:1-2 ESV).
[82] (Al Ahzab 71).

Acknowledging our Creator even without witnessing Him, then worshipping Him. God says in the *Quran*, "Did you think that We created you in vain, and that to Us you will not be returned?"[83] in addition to: "We did not create the heavens and the earth and what lies between them except with reason, and for a finite period. But the blasphemers continue to ignore the warnings they receive."[84]

It is similarly written in *The Old Testament*, "The LORD by wisdom founded the earth; by understanding he established the heavens". [85] This is in line with what Park and Pargament concluded – that religion provides an insight into the purpose of our existence and our significance.[86]

The Magnifying Glass Focuses Meanings Together

Living life with the perspective of faith is a gift, granted by the Creator; and all the meanings of this life are a gift, bestowed with the aim of testing us. Believers think that acknowledging *the* Giver of these gifts is their path to the ultimate reward of being immortal in what their souls have desired. However,

---

[83] (al-Mu'minun 115).

[84] (al-Ahqaf 3).

[85] (Proverbs 3:19 ESV).

[86] C. L. Park, 'Religion as a meaning-making framework in coping with life stress', Journal of Social Issues, vol. 61, no. 4, 2005, pp. 707-729.

whoever denies and rejects these gifts shall be condemned; "We guided him to the way, be he appreciative or unappreciative"[87] and in the *Old Testament*, "for those who honour me I will honour, and those who despise me shall be lightly esteemed".[88]

Faith gathers all the meanings of our lives in the basket of testing; money and offspring are the adornments that render life more beautiful. God says in the noble *Quran*, "Wealth and children are the adornments of the present life"[89] and in *The New Testament*, "God, who richly provides us with everything to enjoy".[90] Money and offspring are also a legacy from *the* Generous One; as God says in the noble Quran, "And provide you with wealth and children, and allot for you gardens, and allot for you rivers".[91]

Offspring is a gift from the Creator; "We created you— if only you would believe! Have you seen what you ejaculate? Is it you who create it, or are We the Creator?"[92] and in *The Old Testament*, "Behold, children are a heritage from the Lord".[93]

---

[87] (al-Insan 3).

[88] (1 Samuel 2:30 ESV).

[89] (Al-Kahf 46).

[90] (1 Timothy 6:17 ESV).

[91] (Nuh 12).

[92] (Al-Waqi'ah 57-59).

[93] (Psalm 127:3 ESV).

The pleasurable food we consume is God's handiwork. We sow and plough, but the original creation is something else; God says in the *Quran*, "Have you seen what you cultivate? Is it you who make it grow, or are We the Grower?" [94] and in *The Old Testament*, "he who gives food to all flesh". [95]

These meanings that we are blessed with - all our money, offspring and meanings of life - are but a trial; "Your possessions and your children are a test, but with God is a splendid reward". [96]

The trial is allotted with the aim of rendering the test tougher and more challenging; for whoever doesn't own much will be more prepared for worshipping God. Meanwhile, a trader's possessions could distract him from worshipping God, and his purpose orientation could shift from desiring God to chasing money.

This is why the test is hard; due to the challenging means of testing that believers faced and still face. God says in the *Quran*, "We have tested those before them. God will surely know the truthful, and He will surely know the liars." [97] A faithful believer will direct all of his aspirations to God and to pleasing Him –

---

[94] (Al-Waqi'ah 63-64).
[95] (Psalm 136:25 ESV).
[96] (At-Taghabun 15).
[97] (Al-'Ankabut 3, The Quran).

including how he raises his children. He shall raise them as his faith dictates.

A faithful person sacrifices money, which God has commanded to be given to the poor and the needy.

God says in the *Quran*, "And they feed, for the love of Him, the poor, and the orphan, and the captive. We only feed you for the sake of God. We want from you neither compensation, nor gratitude"[98] and in *The Old Testament*, "For there will never cease to be poor in the land. Therefore, I command you, 'You shall open wide your hand to your brother, to the needy and to the poor, in your land."[99] It shall not be that one person's riches greatly increase, whereas the poor barely find any food to eat.

The same concept applies to all the meanings that constitute their tests; for they should express their gratitude for them first, and carry out their duty towards them next. Hood mentions that religion provides a universal meaning; for it is sufficient to count as a comprehensive meaning for all meanings, and as an easy and facilitated introduction to ethics, customs, education and social relationships. The solutions offered by religion profoundly tackle people's interests in exploring what is beyond the visible reality.

---

[98] (Al-Insan 8, The Quran)
[99] (Deuteronomy 15:11 ESV).

Faith Knows Achievement and Excellence

Believers see achievement and excellence from new angles, eternal life in Paradise is the achievement:

"He who is drawn away from the Fire and admitted to Paradise has attained [his desire]. And what is the life of this world except the enjoyment of delusion"[100] and in *The New Testament*: "I have come that they may have life, and that they may have it more abundantly".[101] Faith makes them see life as the test room, and all the choices they choose they see as the test questions, and everything that happens in the test room, cannot be as great as the test outcome. They believe that glory and prestige in this life is not important if there is humiliation in the Hereafter, but if it is glory in this life together with glory in the Hereafter, then that is what their Lord ordered them to follow, God says in the *Qur'an*, "But seek, through that which God has given you, the home of the Hereafter; and [yet], do not forget your share of the world. And do good as God has done good to you. And desire not corruption in the land.

Indeed, God does not like corrupters." Similarly in *The Old Testament*: "Behold, that which I have seen good, which is good: for man to eat and drink and see good from all his labours ... the

---

[100] (Al-Imran: 185).
[101] (John 10:10 ESV).

days of his life".[102] The meaning of their lives does not depend on their social status or the value of their property or the value of their wealth, these matters are not among the test questions, they see them as tools to complete the test. Believers who practice religion see wealth, status, properties and influence the way a traveller who is travelling on sea or on land sees the food he is carrying to aid him reach his destination, the travellers know that the borders of the country they want to enter do not allow entry with any luggage, or food, and they leave the land without taking any baggage with them as well. They are pursuing this life in order to reach the Hereafter, and when they are begrudging in this life, it is to maximize the results of their test, they get more wealth to spend more on good deeds. Believers look at both lives as two journeys. The first journey is an hour long and filled with turbulence, and the second journey they will never step out of, they believe that the one-hour journey does not deserve to be given a great deal of weight. To fight for a better position, post or service, departing from it is quick and aiming for it is fruitless. No matter what faces them in terms of lack of money or illness or unfairness, they are confident that God will compensate them for what they have suffered.

The lenses of faith marginalize the achievements they receive, for all are perishable, and the highest value is the Hereafter. God

---

[102] (Ecclesiastes 5:18)

113

says in the *Qur'an*, "But you prefer the worldly life, While the Hereafter is better and more enduring" [103] and in *The Old Testament*, "You will guide me with Your counsel, And afterward receive me to glory." [104] Faith reorganizes the reward of achievements, for some to be an immediate reward and some for the afterlife, a good life in this world is among the immediate rewards in the *Qur'an*: "Whoever does righteousness, whether male or female, while he is a believer – We will surely cause him to live a good life, and We will surely give them their reward [in the Hereafter] according to the best of what they used to do." [105] Security and shelter are also the immediate rewards in the *Old Testament*: "The beloved of the Lord shall dwell in safety by Him, Who shelters him all the day long; And he shall dwell between His shoulders" [106] and there are many immediate rewards such as blessings, health, devotion of children, longevity and many more, while the afterlife rewards are eternity in what the soul desires. God says in the *Quran*: "they are, in that which their souls desire, abiding eternally" and in *The Old Testament*: "Everyone who is found written in the book... shall awake, Some to everlasting life" [107] and that is the achievement "And

---

[103] (Al A'la 16-17).
[104] (Psalm 73:24 ESV).
[105] (Al-Nahl 97).
[106] (Deuteronomy 33:12 ESV).
[107] (Daniel 12:1-2 ESV).

whoever obeys Allah and His Messenger has certainly attained a great attainment".[108]

Faith has a Meaning for Evil

The believers who practice religion in their lives trust in God's compensation to them when calamities happen. They review the events of their lives when the calamities hit them and revisit the words of God.

Muslims find in the *Holy Quran* the words of God: "Indeed, the patient will be given their reward without account"[109] and the Jews and Christians find in *The Old Testament*: "I will restore to you the years that the swarming locust has eaten".[110] Therefore the faith in the coming compensation makes them able to see the meaning of the bad events and the implications, and when calamities come, the meaning of compensation which Muslims see makes them more prepared for calamities and better able to deal with them and it brings them less psychological damage. They believe that their benefits in this life are realized and not postponed until after death, faith brings them psychological balance and dismisses despair, frustration and the bad feelings which result from the calamity. The researcher Park concluded in his research dated 2007, that the religious framework

---

[108] (Al Ahzab 71).

[109] (Az Zumar 10).

[110] (Joel 25:2 ESV).

115

contributes to the ability of the believers to deal with the various pressures of life.

The School of Evil

The calamity might be clear evil to the unbelievers, but for believers, calamities enrol them in 'the school of evil', where they learn how God has a will that is different from their will. In it they study what he wants for them, and in that school, they learn to search for the Creator's messages beneath the 'stones' of their misfortunes. God says in the *Quran*: "And whatever strikes you of disaster – it is for what your hands have earned; but He pardons much"[111] and in *The Old Testament*: "For it is better, if it is the will of God, to suffer for doing good than for doing evil".[112] Therefore, believers see a beautiful meaning for the worse events, it is natural for them to see the beautiful meanings in the days of prosperity and pleasure, when they feel that the creator of the universe is with them, supports them, protects them, honours them, drives evil away from them and delights them. When believers see the beauty in their unpleasant events, the bad events turn into positive events. It leads them to enhance the overall meaning of their lives, and the meanings of bad events are like black pearl beads, and the meanings of the beautiful events are white pearl beads, both make the necklace of 'their lives' meanings'. It leads to organized, beautiful and

---

[111] (Ash shura 30).
[112] (1 Peter 3:17 ESV).

harmonious meanings, and makes the meaning stand in all moments when believers put on the lenses of faith.

The Meanings of Calamities

The believers' loss of their children or loved ones, or the losing of their property or money in a calamity or misfortune, makes them come out of the box of their lives and reconsider it outside its previous events. They re-evaluate when they create the link between the events and the knowledge and approval of God. God says in the *Quran*: "And with Him are the keys of the unseen; none knows them except Him. And He knows what is on the land and in the sea. Not a leaf falls but that He knows it" [113] and in *The Old Testament*: "God … who is perfect in knowledge" [114] and therefore the believers feel psychological comfort, when they restore the internal balance of the feelings of discomfort resulting from the loss, because the compensation for them is assured and guaranteed. And when they re-evaluate the events, they reconsider the reason why God takes from them what He has given them, they are confident that God does not need what he has taken from them, so what is the reason of taking without need?

Believers know that God does not start evil, God is pure good, God says in the *Quran*: "God is the Light of the heavens and the

---

[113] (Al-An'am 59).
[114] (Job 37:15-16 ESV).

earth"[115] and in the *Old Testament*: "You are good, and do good;"[116] and when they see evil in the events of their calamities, they attribute it to their shortcomings and sins. In the Holy Quran, "Corruption has appeared throughout the land and sea by [reason of] what the hands of people have earned so He may let them taste part of [the consequence of] what they have done that perhaps they will return [to righteousness]"[117] and also, "and what comes to you of evil, [O man], is from yourself"[118] and in *The Old Testament*: "The integrity of the upright will guide them, But the perversity of the unfaithful will destroy them"[119] and also "But as for you, you meant evil against me; but God meant it for good".[120]

Believers believe that their Lord is the one who gives the sinners their punishment in this life or postpones it to the afterlife, God says in the *Quran* about postponement of punishment: "And if God were to impose blame on the people for what they have earned, He would not leave upon the earth any creature. But He defers them for a specified term"[121] and in *The Old Testament*: "If the righteous will recompensed on the earth, How much more

---

[115] (An Nur 35).

[116] (Psalm 119:68 ESV).

[117] (Ar Rum 41).

[118] (An Nisa 79).

[119] (Proverbs 11:3 NKJV).

[120] (Genesis 50:20 NKJV).

[121] (Fatir 45).

the ungodly and the sinner" [122] and this context makes the emotions of believers enflame with a fear of God Almighty, and love for God, the Bountiful, the Generous and the provider of blessing: "That is the bounty of Allah, which He gives to whom He wills, and Allah is the possessor of great bounty"[123] and in *The New Testament*: "God, who gives to all liberally and without reproach"[124] and the more love and fear there is in the hearts of the believers, the more they know God and his actions, "Only those fear God, from among His servants, who have knowledge"[125] and in *The Old Testament*: "I am a Hebrew; and I fear the Lord, the God of heaven, who made the sea and the dry land". [126]

Believers know that God is reminding them of his existence and his power, "I'm the only One who can remove the calamities", their lenses of faith show them the link between the calamity and their sins and shortcomings. When calamity comes to them, they rethink their relationships with their families, their parents and their children and remember God's orders to them to be good to neighbours, and to maintain kinship ties or spend their money on goods, they review their mistakes and re-evaluate their faith and

---

[122] (Proverbs 11:31 NKJV).

[123] (Al Jumu'ah 4).

[124] (James 1:5).

[125] (Fatir 28) .

[126] (Jonah 1:9 NKJV).

wonder how this life kept them too busy for his obedience and the commitment to his orders. Calamities are in their nature 'calamitous'. Even the most faithful will be affected by them, but my point is, when you believe that God sent the calamity for a reason, there is benefit in the search for that reason. Despite the heartache or the pain, there is the opportunity also to grow and better ourselves.

Spiritual Meanings in Evil

Religion is about trust and belief, some believers trust in their Lord, absolute trust, and they practice their religion to its fullest, and some trust in their Lord as they trust their friends, indeed they trust them, however, not to the extent of giving them power over their properties for example. Some believers do not want to give their Lord authority over their lives and events due to weakness in their faith, and when the calamities come, they will review the events of their lives away from the bonds of faith and the divine messages, thus may lose the feeling of comfort which results from their confidence in compensation, or their feeling of comfort might be delayed, but believers who practice religion see the messages within their bad incidents. Despite the degree of the calamity they feel relieved that God is speaking to them through His actions, it reminds them of his presence and guides them to the more righteous path. Calamities are God's will and wisdom in the testing, God wants them to re-evaluate the direction of their lives. When they re-evaluate the events of their lives, they will feel pressures resulting from the calamity and the self-criticism that accompanies it. Perhaps that is the explanation of what the researcher Park put forward (2005)[127] that believers are subjected to greater psychological pressure when they lose loved ones, they experience contradiction in understanding their calamity as a result of their assessment in the context of their religious system, and after several months, the pressures disappear and are reversed for the relationship in the long-term to become positive.

The Feelings That Result from Speaking to the Creator

Believers reach the meanings of their lives in the worst conditions of calamities. These meanings, which many believers see are great in number, but the most beautiful among them is 'knowing that God approved it', and God knows what is best for the and He chooses for them better than their choosing for themselves. God says in the *Holy Quran*: "Had God known any good in them, He would have made them hear"[128] and in *The Old Testament*: "Before I was afflicted I went astray, But now I keep Your word."[129]

God sees the true results of their tests in this life and urges them to achieve high results by His actions, for them to be in higher ranks in the afterlife. God says in the *Holy Quran*: "And hasten to forgiveness from your Lord and a garden as wide as the

---

[127] Park, 2005, *op.cit.*

[128] (Al Anfal 23).

[129] (Psalm 119:67 NKJV).

heavens and earth, prepared for the righteous,"[130] and in *The New Testament*: "For it is better, if it is the will of God, to suffer for doing good than for doing evil"[131]

The lens of faith shows the believers orderliness in the most random matters, they see illness as test, their patience, satisfaction and all the desires of their hearts is subject to testing, therefore, they choose to accept calamities, and they move away from anxiety, despair and frustration. God says in the *Holy Quran*: "And whoever is patient and forgives – indeed, that is of the matters [requiring] determination". [132] Also in the *New Testament*: "Indeed we count them blessed who endure. You have heard of the perseverance of Job and seen the end intended by the Lord". [133]

Faith makes frustrations as doubting the ability of their Lord to repair the coming matters, and makes them clean the lens of their faith to help them see 'the light in the illness tunnel or calamity'. Therefore, they feel that they are closer to the Lord, "And [mentions] Job, when he called to his Lord, 'Indeed, adversity has touched me, and you are the Most Merciful of the merciful."[134] Also in *The New Testament*: "Blessed is the man

---

[130] (Imran 133).

[131] (1 Peter 3:17 NKJV).

[132] (Ash Shura 43).

[133] (James 5:11 NKJV).

[134] (Al Anbiya 83)

who endures temptation; for when he has been approved, he will receive the crown of life which the Lord has promised to those who love Him".[135]

Does Faith Provide Appropriate Meaning?

Yes indeed.

An Appropriate Form That Combines Inconsistencies

Faith provides the test theory that makes matters more logical. When it explains suffering, it clarifies that suffering is brief and temporary for believers, their current lives are short, and their complete lives are free of pain, sorrow, and without any suffering, and their version of life which is under experiment is not that important. Therefore, trust in the afterlife makes suffering unimportant for believers and makes suffering inflated (exaggerated) for non-believers, those who do not believe in an afterlife will see that their only version of life, for they have no other is filled with misery, distress, weakness, disease and suffering, and they have no means of reforming it.

Faith offers suffering as an important motive (among other motives) that makes humans aspire to eternal life that is without flaws, and the Creator alone is able to give the 'eternal' version of life which will be a complete life, designed to have pleasure

---

[135] (James 1:12 NKJV)

and indulgence in paradise, and those who want to have that life and the gifts that comes with it, they should thank the giver of the first life opportunity and recognize their Creator, and that He is God who has no equal or equivalent and all His creatures must bow to Him, worship and sanctify Him.

An Appropriate Leader for the Meanings of Life's Band

I was preceded in this idea by Baumeister (1991), when he said that meanings of life have the same kind of meaning as the meaning of a sentence in a few important ways: the parts fit together in a coherent pattern and into a broader context and both are capable of being understood by others and invoke shared assumptions, [136] as I have also been preceded by researcher Hood (2009) when he said that religion is uniquely capable of providing a global meaning and is capable of forming a comprehensive meaning for all meaning systems[137].

Faith is an excellent leader for the meaning of life's band, transforming all events of our lives into instruments that play in harmony, and combines meanings in a container of experiments and tests. Faith resonates meanings in the meaning of life's band, and makes beautiful meanings harmonize with the love of the Giver of those meanings, as faith also makes the drums of

---

[136] R. F. Baumeister, *Meanings of Life*, Guilford, New York, NY, 1991.
[137] R. W. Hood Jr., P. C. Hill, B. Spilka, *The Psychology of Religion*, 4th edn., An empirical approach, Guilford Press, New York, 2009.

"misfortune" harmonize with the rhythm of the music of prosperity. Faith is able to make us see aesthetics of misfortunes, despite all the inconveniences of unfortunate events.

The believers 'alone' are able to make all the events of their lives be harmonized with the tones of musical instruments. Misfortunes, suffering, pain, sadness and separation from loved ones are instruments which have no function for non-believers. They believe it produces unpleasant sounds, while believers make these instruments harmonize with the rhythm of their lives - as we have mentioned in the school of evil – and they are experts in using these events and its meanings to play within the meanings of their lives' band.

To summarize, all events in our lives are an instrument, some will be melodic and some will be discordant. The believers will be able to use their 'lens of faith' to put all these instruments together to create a tune that is beautiful, that is easy on the ear. Non-believers will only hear their melodic instruments, interrupted by the discordant noise of those instruments created by life's calamities.

When faith leads the actions of believers in their social interactions, it leads to tolerance, forgiveness and patience, as morality is the shortest way to please God and remain eternally in His heavens. When faith leads a believer's business transactions, it will lead them to integrity, honesty and honouring contracts and covenants. Faith will lead believers to be faithful in their marriages, to fulfil their responsibilities, and raise their children. In their occupations, faith will lead them to be committed, and protect the rights of others, or the rights of those who they work for or those who work for them, as honest earnings is among the basics of faith, these are only examples, as faith covers all aspects of life and leads believers to be better.

An Appropriate Light Reveals the Vision and Mission

In recent years, business management activities have developed in a very big way. Success in the business world is very complex and requires a complex system that fits the needs and details of each department and the tasks it carries out so that it results as a business activity, where its various bodies operate in a compatible and harmonious way. These activities present a very large goal which companies call 'the mission', and there is 'the vision' and it is the position where businesses aspire to see themselves in the future. What the giant companies are doing is to try to turn factories, offices and people, all these individual factors, into a single harmonious body.

The responsibility of the president of this company and its senior management is to share with all employees the mission and vision that is prepared for them. They prepare the annual goals for them so it works like a body with its harmonious systems. Our hearts, lungs and digestives systems all work together for the 'mission' of sustaining healthy life. It is absolutely coherent, the more harmony there is, the more the goals are achieved and the more the returns become higher.

Investors in corporate shares know this fact very well, some companies have a lot of assets and resources, however the risk of its failure is high if the company does not have a vision which it sees and seeks the future. It might fail as the pioneer company as Polaroid did, which introduced in 1943 the instant photos. At the time it was an incredible thing, previously the extraction of images took days. In those times you had to send the film to a laboratory for processing, and Polaroid gained a huge profit from this invention which lasted for decades. The reasons for its failure was due to the vision of its chief executive officer in 1985. He developed the wrong concept for the company when he sent a message to the company's employees telling them that 'keeping photos in a 'tangible' and visual album is a basic need for all people and because the ultimate goal of the company became wrong at the time, the company did not survive in the business world, and that is what researchers at Yale School of Management have proven.[138] Time proved that there is no need for an old photo album, and people are no longer in need of them.

Faith offers believers the great goal, they set goals for their current lives and long-term goals for the afterlife, they want their share of this life and they want their share of the hereafter life. These goals will not allow human beings to feel failure, all

---

[138] businessinsider.com/10-brands-that-committed-suicide-2013-3#polaroid-7 (Accessed 13-10-2017)

127

losses in this life cannot be compared to the loss of eternal life. Researchers concluded that a goal is one of the components of the meaning of life, and when faith guides them to see the greater meaning of their existence in this life, and it is to pass the test and then be in paradise eternally, believers will not end their lives for financial loss, the loss of a loved one or devastating illness. The journey is still ongoing, their tests are ongoing, and the goal has not been achieved yet.

A Container Appropriate for all the Details

Faith suits the rich billionaires, and drives them to be kind to the poor and help the needy, they know the more their money grows, the harder the test gets. Believers know that their money is part of their test, and the poor with all their needs, weaknesses and suffering, speak to their Lord in all their conditions. With the continuation of prayers and talking to God every day, they feel God is getting closer to them. They find that God's compensation for their patience is determined, the rich want eternity in paradise, the same as the poor; even the disabled and the sick find in their faith a comfort for their hearts and a relief from their pain.

Children will recognize their Lord as they begin to recognize their lives and its events. The youth will find that their instincts are at their most intense and ambition is at its highest level, and they want a shorter path (it might be the wrong path) to achieve their goals, but faith motivates them to be patient and enduring, keeping them from falling and preserves the society as a whole.

When we get older our taste for enjoying things becomes different, faith give us the ultimate joy that fits that stage when we become closer to meeting God. Older people's bodies may not be fit for entertainment and movement, illness might disable them, friends may desert them, and they feel lonely, but the feelings of being close to their Creator will comfort them. Believers have spent their lives being closer to God and are waiting for the moment when they will meet Him, and to look at His face after they die. It will make them feel inner satisfaction whenever they read His words. Their feelings are the feelings of a child who abandoned his moneybox and left his sweets, believers who grow in their faith will open the moneybox of their charitable deeds soon, and meet with their loved ones who have left them.

Faith is appropriate for all the stages of human ages, introducing virtuous morality in childhood, showing youth the limits of their behaviour, reminding adults of their mission and the purpose of their existence, and comforting us with the feeling of being closer to God in our old age. It is appropriate for the idea of death, and makes death more positive as it is a meeting with the Creator. It is appropriate for all people with all their functions. A judge who is a believer is motivated by his faith to work hard and investigate cases. Faith motivates him to judge fairly, the accountant fears the great judgment day, and a teacher hopes to say a word which improves the situation of a student and elevates his charitable deeds in the Hereafter. That is faith and its influences, we will find its impact on all peoples' domains, and specialties at all ages.

Appropriate Remedy for Littleness

Humans may forget that they are on a small planet which is no more than a point in the vast sea of the universe, when we compare our lifespan of up to 100 years with the age of the universe, which is 13 billion years old. We then are aware of just how short our lives are, we remember that we are one person out of the 7 billion people living with us on this planet. In every 100 years, only a few will remain from the billions, billions of lives will come after ours and there are billions which came before us, and the lives of those among us who will live 100 years will not be a complete hundred years of life filled with enjoyment. Its pleasures will be reduced by sleep, intermixed with grief, the remaining will be consumed by diseases and the rest of its days will be filled with hard work, fatigue and misery. Life clearly has lots of good moments too, it's a balance. There will of course be laughter, happy memories, love, kindness, compassion and lots of beauty to appreciate. How tiny we are, weak, few and strangers to most. Believers see faith as their remedy, which gives them life without current imperfection.

An Appropriate Context for all Sciences

The single cell that made a genetic leap two billion years ago created us. Our little dwelling on the surface of a tiny planet which hardly appears in the map of this vast universe was built by gravity 13 billion years ago. Our food are plants that have grown from algae and ferns to turn into seed plants started 450 million years ago.[141] That is the context of science, while faith provides these same scientific facts but in a more logical context.

Our existence is not a coincidence and random, it is God's will that determined how we will exist, and when, and created plants' mechanisms because He willed our existence and that is our food, and the universe is very, very, very massive, so that He shows us His power, greatness and glory. He puts the sun in its orbit to wake us up in the morning, and sets it at night for us to sleep, "Are you a more difficult creation or is the heaven? God constructed it, He raised its ceiling and proportioned it, And He[139] darkened its night and extracted its brightness, And after that He spread the earth, He extracted from it its water and its pasture, And the mountains He set firmly, As provision for you and your grazing livestock",[140] and in *The Old Testament* "In the beginning God created the heavens and the earth."[141]

This is an example of the context of science in faith's perspective, although this subject is filled with information and examples and can be a fertile field to talk about.

---

[139] C. H. Wellman, P. L. Osterloff, U. Mohiuddin, 'Fragments of the earliest land plants', *Nature,* vol. 425, no. 6955, 2003, pp. 282–285.

[140] SAHIHINTERNATIONAL,http://www.alquranenglish.com/quransurah-an-naziat-33-qs-79-33-in-arabic-and-english-translation

[141] (Genesis 1:1 NKJV)

An Appropriate Fit to My Standard

My previous book *5 Essential Dimensions* is based on the premise that the universe is balanced, and that living plants are balanced, and the stars move in balanced routes. Our solar system is also balanced, and the location of the Sun is balanced. If the Sun got even slightly closer to us, its radiation would burn us. Even our internal world, our organs and everything we deal with consists of balanced atoms moving in its nucleus in a balanced way. When we get diseases, we get to treat them, then when we know how their system works, there is a clear and fixed balance. In my previous book, I provided a hypothesis that balance for us as human beings does exist, but if we lose it, we only need to look for the obstacles of balance. Based on that hypothesis and some other hypotheses, *5 Essential Dimensions* is a system that shows us the five dimensions of our lives, and when we deal properly with those five dimensions, our lives will be balanced.

We are an integral part of this balanced universe. We will be balanced after we lift the obstacles of balance, and today, I will not repeat my previous discussion about the balance of the universe, as it is well established, and revealed by the mighty binoculars that show us the edges of the distant universe. This balance has been proven by the magnified microscopes that show us the elements of living cells and even the atoms of these elements.

When I searched for the meaning of life I was looking for the perfect meaning which I found in the perfection of the atoms in the nucleus, in the perfect rotation of the stars, and in the perfect laws of physics that order the work of galaxies. I searched for the meaning of life that fits the breath-taking beauty of life that I find by looking at the sky, and the lights of the stars, the beauty I find in the attractiveness of flowers, and its perfume carried on the wind; the beauty of ocean's fishes; the rose fields; and the view of clouds from the window of an airplane. Life's beauty and perfection are the minimum parts of the meaning of life, whatever was the logic that made us alive, whatever is the meaning of life, it will not dismiss the meaning of life to be the logic of things, the logic that brought us to the treasures of experimental sciences, made our watches talk, our blind see, and our mute talk. It's the logic that taught us how to extract treasures from the earth, how to build skyscrapers, and provided us with warm meals at altitudes of 41 thousand feet.

Logic is what guided us to fields of research, and it is what leads brainstorming and the exchange of ideas and discussions. This perfect logic is what I searched for, I wanted to see the logic behind the science that measures everything, weighs it, describes it, causes it, and searches for solutions. I want to see it as I have known it, measuring, weighing and describing our life, and then causing its existence with the same perfection. I searched for perfection that makes the meaning of our lives coherent, as the arithmetic result of $1 + 1 = 2$ which is something that cannot be disputed or doubted, and is not open to interpretation.

Here I am finding in faith what I was looking for which showed me the signature of the master who I know very well from the beauty of the universe, its perfection and the logic of things, and from my book *5 Essential Dimensions* which was based on that. As each artist signs his paintings after completing them, I found in faith the signature of the master, the beauty of the beautiful, the greatness of the great and the magnificence of the logic in granting life under conditions of experiment and testing.

Chapter 6

Q & A

Q: In my opinion, the theory of evolution is in conflict with religion. If religion is meant to show a meaning in life, how could we accept what is in conflict with the asserted scientific facts?

A: The theory of evolution requires a thorough explanation which cannot be reviewed in this book, because it is not part of my account of the meaning of life. Briefly speaking, the theory of evolution accounts for the mechanism by which man has evolved from other living beings. It was proposed by Charles Darwin, and offers an explanation for the gradual evolution of man from pre-human ancestors.

This is not the only theory in literature that explains the evolution of man; there are two other theories. In their theory of *Punctuated Equilibrium*, Stephen Jay Gould (Harvard University) and Niles Eldredge (University of Columbia) have proposed a different mechanism for the evolutionary process, arguing that a key feature in most evolution is long periods of stability, which are infrequently interrupted by rapid periods of branching evolution. Gould and Eldredge supported their position with evidence collected from the fossil records. [142] Another theory, that of *Catastrophism*, originated by Georges Cuvier, proposes that the Earth had largely been shaped by sudden, short-lived, violent events. Such catastrophes would be a much more immediate force for change of the world than Darwin's slow evolution.

Such a diversity of theories of evolution show that the mechanism by which man has evolved has not been settled by a single theory. The door of science is open to more hypotheses that could account for the mechanism of man's evolution.

The view I provide on the origin of humanity is irrelevant to the book's general aim, which is bringing religions to a consensus. The story of the creation of Adam (the father of all human beings) by God is not identical in the holy books of the different religions I surveyed. However, I will not go beyond what I know about the story of creation from the Islamic perspective, for I am limited to my own knowledge.

The Islamic version goes like this: God created Adam and commanded His angels to prostrate to him. All angels prostrated - except Satan, who objected and refused to do so; for he

---

[142] Wikipedia contributors, 'Punctuated Equilibrium', Wikipedia The Free Encyclopedia, [website], last edited 2017, https:// en.wikipedia.org/wiki/Punctuated_equilibrium, (accessed 1 October 2017).

claimed to be better than man: God "said, 'O Satan, what prevented you from prostrating before what I created with My Own hands? Are you too proud, or were you one of the exalted?'"[143] Muslim theologians refer to God's words "what I had created with My Own hands" as of significance to God's direct execution of creation and concluded Adam is created separately from all other animals (this idea is supported in additional Islamic texts). Meanwhile, God has mentioned in another instance in the *Quran* that He has created cattle with His own hands: "Have they not seen that We created for them, of Our Handiwork, livestock that they own!" [144] Despite this statement, it is clear that intentional cattle-breeding is the work of human enterprise and ingenuity rather than God's direct action on the world.

Therefore, the implicit meaning of the theory of evolution (that God has, at most, "indirectly" created man) needs some more research by theologians. The *Quran cannot* be wrong, and it is beyond all question. The holy *Quran* is preserved in the original form, all versions that are 1400 years old are identical, and God has asserted that he will save it as it is without changes. In this, I agree with what Galileo Galilei said: "Holy Scripture and nature are both emanations from the divine word: the former dictated

---

143 (Saad: 75).
144 (YaSin: 71).

137

by the Holy Spirit, the latter the observant executrix of God's commands."[145]

Regarding the conflict between science and religious scriptures that relate to the mechanism of the creation of man, this could be attributed to a group of factors, not including the invalidity of religion. One of these factors is the misinterpretation of scriptural texts by theologians – not to mention their pre-existing insights. Such an error does not accuse theologians of ill intention, but rather a recognition of our limited minds' failing attempts to visualize written texts.

Because our predecessors did not have the broad spectrum of sciences that we have today, their visualizations of the scriptures were restricted by the amount of knowledge they had back then. Religions are like a water stream;[146] the closer they are to the source of the message, the cleaner the water is to drink. We are ages away from the era of divine messages, and thus, the subsequent generations have contributed with their own commentaries of the scriptures, not all of which may be as absolutely perfect as the original.

I see no evident contradiction in the texts of the *Quran* in Islam.

_____

[145] M. Caputo, Galileo: Atheist or Believer in God?, http://atheismexposed.tripod.com/galileo_and_god.htm#_edn9, 2005, (accessed 14 September 2017).

[146] Cited from a verbal conversation with Abdul Latif Al Muslim.

Nevertheless, they require researchers and theologians to exert tremendous efforts on re-visiting these texts in light of scientific facts. One such text in the noble *Quran* is "And Allah has created every animal[147] from water. Of them are some that go upon their bellies, and of them are some that go upon two feet, and among them are some that go upon four. Allah creates what He pleases. Surely, Allah has the power to do all that He pleases."[148] Such a text suggests more of a continuity between the world's many animals, and such would point in the direction of an evolutionary theory.

Q: Is the concept of man evolving from pre-human beings consistent with the paradigm and statutes of religion?

A: The concept of evolution is *not* consistent with the concepts of dominion and superiority that make us feel superior to and distinguished from other creatures. In contrast, the idea of evolution is consonant with the idea that human beings are undergoing a test, in particular one in which the main subject of evaluation is acknowledging the Creator without witnessing him.

The idea of human beings evolving from pre-human ancestors

---

[147] According to As-Saadi Quran commentary of Surat Hud, verse 6, an "animal" is whatever steps on the ground, be it human, wild animal or sea animal. As-Saadi, Commentary of the Noble Quran, http://quran.ksu.edu.sa/tafseer/saadi/sura11-aya6.html, [website], (accessed 15-9-2017).
[148] (Hud :6).

will not alter the fact that God has meant for us to undergo the test of acknowledging Him without having any "experimental" proof of his direct intervention in the process of creation. In other words, our test will remain without any hints of any kind, except those which God wanted to provide as evidence of His existence. The more strictly-controlled the test room is, the more accurate the test outcomes are. If God wanted to leave a clue guiding us to a tangible proof of His existence, then the test of His acknowledgment would be annulled; it'd not be a test but rather a simple recitation.

A solid proof that could lead us to God's existence, and bring us to the certainty that blind evolution is insufficient does not actually exist. If everyone came to know God through an ultimate, testable proof, this would be similar to cheating in an exam, and would result in discrediting the hypothesis of the test, as well as dispensing with the need to test the participants at all; for they have already known the answer to the main test question. Hence, there would be no more need for a "test," which is the basis of any religion that calls for faith in what is unseen.

Thus, settling on an experimental proof about God without reading His word and acknowledging Him is something that God did not desire. Therefore, our existence as a result of evolution is an added control to the room of our test.

Evolution, with all its concepts, only explains the mechanism of development – and nothing more. It does not indicate what started evolution or what determined its process. Explaining these are still open for the work of religious thinkers. Religions are not supposed to contradict science by any means. It could be that the moment when the truth about God being the Creator will be revealed, through a crucial and conclusive proof, is the moment when the world will come to an end.

There is a *Quran* verse that refers to the timing of the end of the world ("the end of the test"), wherein God says, "Until, when the earth puts on its fine appearance, and is beautified, and its inhabitants think that they have mastered it, Our command descends upon it by night or by day"[149] meaning that when the beauty of the Earth has come to completion and perfection, it will then be the hour when the world ends and the afterlife begins, and for sure, science is capable of bringing the earth to perfection. At this instance, science will have culminated in the point that could lead us all to faith.

Q: There have been countless discourses between religious scientists and atheist scientists about the meaning of life. Why don't we get significant results out of them?

A: I have viewed some of these discourses, and I have noticed that their disputes are about the level of their motives, rather than their claims. In other words, they claim to be objective and

---

[149] (Yunus: 24).

to adhere to a scientific frame. However, their arguments' motives are crystal clear to me, as is their inability to speak only from the position of science.

Some people are sincere seekers of the truth, and admit the truth as non-negotiable. Other people argue in order to make themselves and their names known. Others take issue driven by their atheism; hence, they hate faith and want to refute it, demolish the glory of religion and reconstruct a new glory for atheism, obscured beneath the cover of science.

Let us not forget that the conflict between religion and science is over. Today, whoever abandons the divine commands will neither be condemned to seven years of prison nor burned naked in a market square, as was Giordano Bruno,[150] who was held in confinement from the years 1593 to 1600 AD, on account of the charges that were made against him for holding opinions contrary to the Catholic faith. He was ultimately burned naked in the Campo de' Fiori in Rome in 1600.

Galileo Galilei, "the father of modern science" as referred to by Einstein, was tried for his writings about heliocentrism. His formal sentence was imprisonment, which was then commuted

---

[150]Wikipedia contributors, 'Giordano Bruno', Wikipedia The Free Encyclopedia, [website], last edited 2017, https://en.wikipedia.org/wiki/Giordano_Bruno, (accessed 15 September 2017).

to house arrest.[151] He actually had deep faith and significant relationships with clergymen.

These incidences, as well as many other crimes committed by clergymen over the years, have rendered modern times an optimal opportunity for revenge and vengeance on the side of atheists.

Let us bear in mind that commentaries of faith are but the personal interpretations and views of theologians. If a theologian is narrow-minded, his commentary will be too conservative. Similarly, the depth of knowledge of an enlightened, broad-minded theologian will be as immeasurable as his ignorance. This restricted insight of religious scriptures has changed; the very same church that had once condemned Galileo reprinted all his works in 1741 AD.

Q: I have read through your previous argument about the theory of evolution and I am still confused! What should I do?

A: Read through the intellectual dilemmas once more, and then re-read the argument. If the confusion is still there, ask yourself this: are you convinced of everything your partner does? Are

---

151 Wikipedia contributors, 'Galileo Galilei', Wikipedia The Free Encyclopedia, [website], last edited 2017, https://en.wikipedia.org/wiki/Galileo_Galilei, (accessed 15 September 2017).

you aware of your heart beat, the movements of your stomach, or of any of your bodily functions while you sleep? Are you totally satisfied with your neighbourhood, your career and your friends?

You deal with all these entities without attempting to drive away your confusion regarding their behaviour. The functioning of your internal organs while you sleep is beyond the level of your consciousness. Despite all of that, you are tolerant towards your ignorance in those cases. You fall asleep regardless of what is going on inside your body. None of us is sleep-deprived because of doubts about how our internal organs function. This is what tolerance to ignorance means. Consider another example: none of our friends appeal to us perfectly. But, we are still tolerant to their differing from us. We accept certain things in life because we cannot know everything there is to know, nor can we expect everything to be perfect. If we didn't, we would be constantly worrying and stressed about uncertainty, about the tiniest details of our lives. We use ignorance as a tool to happiness.

And this is how life is in its entirety; much ignorance exists, but we tolerate and ignore it, without letting it perplex us. Let us take from religion what is good, and tolerate our ignorance about some of its aspects. It could be that the science that is more congruent with religion has not come yet.

Q: Three separate, yet similar, questions from three persons who follow three different religions: the first one is from a Muslim who states, "I have learned about Islam, but your arguments in this book have left me perplexed." The second one says, "I am a Christian, and what I was taught at church is not in line with what you pointed out about Christianity. The teachings about trials are not put that way, and it's so confusing." The third exclaims, "I am a Jew who has studied the scripture well, and what you say contradicts what I know."

A: It appears as though your "minds" are like a bowl which hasn't been cleaned before pouring some milk into it; they are dirty and ruin the milk's flavour. I suggest you read through the introduction once more, and, at least temporarily, put aside your pre-learned concepts from religion (just until the end of the book). After experiencing to the full what this book has to offer about the meaning of life, each can revert to prior beliefs.

When we open up, our bowls will be squeaky clean, and we will be able to perceive the real taste of milk. On the contrary, if we just cling to what our bowls are already containing, we will end up tasting a mixture that is pleasant to no one. Using an open mind, purely for the purpose of examining a topic, is in no way letting go of your own beliefs. It simply gives you an unbiased testing ground for new ideas. Then it is of course your own choice whether you take on board any new concepts, or simply revert back to your own way of thinking. But, without an open mind, you will never have the full picture and you won't be giving yourself the chance of a little enlightenment in new areas.

On a final note, this book has presented the meaning of life through evidence based on the *Old Testament* which is equally approved by Judaism and Christianity, in addition to *Quran* texts. A bewildered reader can search into the validity and credibility of these texts and see that they have been correctly cited within their context. I would like to point out that the benefits of this book cannot be fathomed in only one session and a reader will do best through repeated engagement, or, at least, repeated engagement with the meaning of their life.

Q: Does the universe need a Creator?

A: When we wear the lenses of experimental science we will see that the universe is equipped to build itself. However, on the other hand we will see that the only true meaning of life is based on the idea of the existence of a Creator for the universe, and without it there is no meaning for life's existence. It is very peculiar that there is a similarity between the idea of the existence of a creator with the idea of the existence of a meaning to life.

Researchers[152] have proven that the meaning of life is important

---

[152] B. Konkolÿ Thege, A. Staudera and M. S. Koppa, 'Relationship between meaning in life and intensity of smoking: do gender differences exist?' Psychology & Health, vol. 25, no. 5, 2010

to our psychological well-being without proving whether a meaning of life exists or not, but they proved that we have a need for a meaning for our lives, and so is the meaning of life that is presented by this book. It is a clear and specific meaning and can be used to understand our lives and its events, but it is based on the assumption that there is a Creator for the universe. The research did not aim to prove a creator for the universe or otherwise, but we have proven that the idea of the existence of a Creator for the universe will lead us to a clear and specific meaning for the meaning of life which will lead us to our psychological well-being, and therefore, we will take our gain from the existence of the Creator without proving or refuting this idea.

Q: Must I leave science to find a meaning for my life?

A: The mind is that which has brought us to science. It is not science that brought us to the mind, the achievements of science should not put us under the illusion that science is more important than our minds. My book's purpose is to shine light on the angle where science "today" is not working, and we have to learn that science is great and effective but limited, and we have to know the meaning of our presence without insisting that we see galaxies with a lens made by a jeweller. Our minds are able to show us all the options to reach or receive information, which go beyond only scientific inquiry.

Q: I am an atheist, I read the book, I agree that science does not lead me to the meaning of life, but I would like to find the meaning of my life away from worshiping, religion, or religious rituals and rites?

A: Allow me to confirm that the complex questions are the ones that are appropriate for the maturity of our minds and the maturity of our experience, therefore, the right question leads to another question. As we move towards a healthy series of questions, we are moving towards the answer, the answer which we can reach from one question had ended in the nursery stage. I think you have completed the first series in a proper way, as you got to know that atheism does not lead to the meaning of life. Everyone has the right to live in their own way, but if you are curious to know the meaning of your own life, it may be useful to investigate religions. After all, I have argued that the religious outlook is the only one able to give a meaning to lives. If one wishes to investigate my claims, then consider the next proper question: what is religion? It is best to learn about them before making a decision about them. Accurate reading about religions and the story of the devil's rejection to worship might give you some guidance and meanings.

Q: Do you think I have to worship God to receive a possible eternity?

A: Knowing the creator gives us a meaning for our life, certain and not just possible, and the possible eternity to you, is certain to me, and it is an additional reward after death, while the main reward remains to recognize life and its meanings.

Q: I do not believe in God, so how can I believe in His messages and His religion?

A: Believing in God is necessary to believe in His messages. When you choose not to believe in Him or not to believe in His existence, that is your choice, however the absence of faith in your heart will result in the absence of meaning of life from your mind and eyes and the absence of the basket that collects the meaning of your life.

Q: After discussing this with my atheist friend, using your book, he told me that he would not believe in God even if his life loses all its meanings. He says faith to him begins with his conviction in the existence of God and proving it, and then builds his life and its meanings on that faith. But, the meaning of life to be the reason to believe in God, he thinks, is a twisted logical equation and a road which he will not follow. He has said that he will follow the path of science that he knows. What do you think?

A: Our faith in our Creator is similar to our existence in this life, we come to exist, we grow up and we understand, and after that we get to know what is around us. Neither I nor even your friend can set the rules of "Life's School" that we have just entered, and we will leave soon. This school was established billions of years ago, and will remain as long as God wills. He (your friend) is standing at the door of the School of Life and wants it to amend its laws for him to enter, I do not agree that his standing by its door is a logical choice. He is unable to see an obvious fact; he is missing that he came from nonexistence to be alive. He speaks, sees and hears, so let him wonder about his fast existence and fast departure as he is wondering about the laws of the school when he stands by its door. But, even if I agree that science will resolve the existence of God one day, are we able to wait for science to resolve the existence of God? For a man who lives a full life may only have 100 years available to wait. What if science discovers God in a million years' time? It's certainly a big gamble waiting for this to happen in your own lifetime!

Q: Religions promise that God is just and merciful, and it is clear to everyone the extent of hatred, injustice and killings that exist in this world. Do you agree that this is a blunt contradiction?

A: The Islamic religion in which I believe does not assume that. God says about the beginning of the existence of man, "And when thy Lord said to the angels: 'I am about to place a vicegerent in the earth,' they said: 'Wilt Thou place therein such as will cause disorder in it, and shed blood? — and we glorify Thee with Thy praise and extol Thy holiness.' He answered: 'I know what you know not.'" Islamic faith differs from other religions, and God has made us humans successors on earth to act as we wish for a limited time.

Q: What are the reasons for your choosing religion to be your interpretation of the meaning of life?

A: If I have found the meaning of life in other sources I wouldn't hide it from you, but the divine messages show that it is the only source of an objective meaning of life, the divine messages present to us the wisdom from God, and this wisdom is found outside our closed life box, whereas philosophy and science are wisdom that comes from within the box.

Q: I am in favour of what you mentioned in your book that the meaning of life cannot come from outside of the framework of religion. I have also accepted that away from the divine messages our life will lose the basket that collects its meaning, but my vision of the meaning of life with the concept of religion is as a result of my vision of God. I want to have a vision of God; how can I have a vision of him? Describe him to me?

A: Here science can serve us, for we are very small in this great universe and certainly God is great. Science tells us that perfection and order exist in the smallest creatures and in the largest of them, and therefore God is a perfect creator, and as for the rest of his qualities, you will find it in all divine messages, and in the *Quran*, which I make sure to read every day.

Q: I am a supporter of most of what you mentioned in your book. How do I invest in the concept of the meaning of life that this book offers, to make the best possible investment?

A: If you agree with most of what is written in this book, you should continue reading holy books. You should also read my book, *5 Essential Dimensions*, [153] which provides the best investment in the meanings of life to reach the goal of reassurance and satisfaction in the five dimensions of our decisions and decision making.

---

[153] A.A.ALEBRAHEEM,5EssentialDimensions,[Amazon], 2016,
https://www.amazon.com/A.A.ALEBRAHEEM/e/B01LMJWH58

About the Author

A. A. Alebraheem is a philosopher, journalist and traveler. He endeavors to answer tough questions on how man exists in various spheres of life: politics, society, philosophy, science, faith and everyday life matters. His first work, "5 Essential Dimensions", covers the topic of how we live. In his second book, "When Life Makes Sense", he gives a straight forward answer to the question of the meaning of life as well as explaining human vision and mission.

He possesses a deep knowledge of the structure of the human mind, based on 35 years of personal reading and research. Alebraheem's writings attempt to see things from alternative angles, searching for patterns and creating successful habits for life. He draws from his life experiences that range from travelling between continents to being a column writer for the well-known Kuwaiti newspaper ALQABAS and guest speaker on Kuwait TV and US radio shows.

Alebraheem also enjoys sharing fresh ideas on his website www.alebraheembooks.com

Other Books

5 ESSENTIAL DIMENSIONS

How to balance your life for health, success and contentment

Life is all about decisions. This book reveals a game-changing new theory to develop decision making maturity. The theory is based on the premise that our lives have five dimensions - the financial, social, internal, physical, and spiritual. We cannot reach our full potential as individuals unless all five of our life dimensions are balanced. If we neglect any of these dimensions, the ensuing disharmony destroys our tranquillity and can wreck our lives.

This book will help you:

- recognize life's five essential dimensions
- master the mechanisms in each dimension
- identify and remove obstacles that prevent balance
- develop methodology in order to make better decisions
- achieve a healthy, balanced, successful and tranquil life

We need to consider the five dimensions in all our decisions in order to live a balanced, successful, and peaceful existence. This refreshing, motivating and persuasive book will help you to keep the five dimensions in balance while making decisions for a better life.

Find on Amazon https://www.amazon.com/dp/B01L9HP0NO

Made in United States
North Haven, CT
25 February 2023

33162680R00088